The
Silicon Eye

BY GEORGE GILDER

The Party That Lost Its Head (with Bruce Chapman)

Men and Marriage

Visible Man

Wealth and Poverty

Recapturing the Spirit of Enterprise

Microcosm

Life After Televsion

Telecosm

The Silicon Eye

The Silicon Eye

George Gilder

Atlas Books

W. W. Norton & Company
New York • London

For information about permission to reproduce selections from this book, write to
Permissions, W. W. Norton & Company, Inc., 500 Fifth Avenue, New York, NY 10110

Manufacturing by The Courier Companies, Inc.
Book design by Chris Welch
Production manager: Amanda Morrison

Library of Congress Cataloging-in-Publication Data

Gilder, George F., date.
The silicon eye / George Gilder.
p. cm. — (Enterprise)
Includes index.
ISBN 0-393-05763-1 (hardcover)
1. Foveon (Firm) 2. High technology industries—California—Santa Clara Valley
(Santa Clara County) 3. Digital electronics. 4. Photography—Digital techniques.
5. Electronic digital computers. 6. Artificial intelligence. 7. Computer vision.
8. Visual perception. 9. Cellular telephones. 10. Mead, Carver. 11. Faggin,
Federico, 1941– I. Title. II. Enterprise (New York, N.Y.)
HC107.C2H5334 2005
338.7'621367'0979473—dc22

2004030994

W. W. Norton & Company, Inc., 500 Fifth Avenue, New York, N.Y. 10110
www.wwnorton.com

W. W. Norton & Company Ltd., Castle House, 75/76 Wells Street, London W1T 3QT

1 2 3 4 5 6 7 8 9 0

For Louisa

Contents

The
Silicon Eye

Carver Mead and Federico Faggin in 1988 in front of a giant model of a microprocessor resembling Faggin's historic designs. At the time, Faggin was CEO and Mead was chairman of Synaptics, a company devoted to creating a new kind of microprocessor inspired by the massively parallel operations of the human brain. Courtesy of Foveon.

Prologue

Who Is Carver Mead?

"**D**eath Valley Nuts and Sweets," beckons the neon sign. Amid the lunar desert rimmed with remote mountains, in a little shop claiming to be "the most beautiful gas station in the world," a sixty-nine year-old man named Carver Mead assumes the iconic pose of the twenty-first-century pilgrim. A trim bearded figure, he is hunched prayerfully among the gas pumps trying to get reception on his cell phone.

The glow from the sign falls on the backseat of his rental car. It is full of arcane century-old technology—an array of apparently random electrical devices that might intrigue a teenaged tinker or strike terror in the mind of an airport security guard. A small middle-aged blond woman sits patiently in the car in front of the electrical debris. She has been through this before.

Who is this Carver Mead, collector of electrical relics? And what is he doing at a dive in the midst of Death Valley in early October 2003, haplessly trying to catch up with the world?

FOLLOWING HIS OWN visions and disciplines, whims and rap-
torial will, Mead has always managed to remain ahead. Although
little known outside the silicon valleys of America, he has been
the leading intellectual figure in four decades of American electronics, through three generations of the fastest-advancing
gauntlet of world technology. Crucial to his lead has been his
intuitive sense of *phase*, his special feel for the timing of the
crests and troughs of opportunity in life and electricity, science
and history. His intuition is nicely summed up in his famous
exhortation, "Listen to the technology; find out what it is telling
you" (meaning to go with the flow of the basic physics rather
than twist it to your own desires).

Born the son of an engineer in a Southern Pacific hydroelec-
tric plant in Kern Valley in California's High Sierras, Mead had
come to learn of the immense power of electricity and the portentous relationships among its phases in the plant. When the
power was in phase, with the crests and troughs aligned between
the generator and the line, electricity would rush reliably down
the eighty miles to Los Angeles. But if the waves of force
between the generator and the transport line were out of phase,
the voltage shift could blow up the plant.

The Gordon and Betty Moore professor of science and engineering at the California Institute of Technology (Caltech), in
Pasadena, Mead early in his career had moved his concerns from
the millions of watts of power in his father's domain to the
nanowatts (billionths of a watt) of power in exotic microelec-
tronic devices. In 1963 he built the world's fastest transistor. He

researched the proposition about the rate of advance of semi-conductor technology, doubling every eighteen months, that he named Moore's Law after its author, Gordon Moore. He conceived the chip design technologies that soon dominated the industry. He proposed and taught a historic course on computational physics with the late Nobel Laureate physicist Richard Feynman, with whom he shared a belief that electromagnetic waves can move both ways in time. He wrote an important book on quantum theory and superconductivity called *Collective Electrodynamics*. Crucial in all these pursuits were phase relationships. Whether the waves of force were in alignment—whether they resonated and grew, or dissipated and dispersed—determined whether useful effects were achieved.

The waves of influence from his classes at Caltech often impelled Mead north to Silicon Valley. From his early years advising Moore at Intel, where Mead wore the seventh badge issued, he spent much of his career commuting to the Bay Area to consult with his students and guide their endeavors. His quiet voice, steady gray eyes, trim goatee, and swirly colored open-necked shirts became familiar in the high councils of the industry. When he says something, you listen. As if to await an alignment of the phases of his thought with yours, he pauses. He thinks before he speaks, and as he thinks he radiates, and the radiation reaches the listener and opens his mind for the impending idea. During the course of his career, many have listened attentively enough to act on his concepts. He has served as a founder of twenty companies.

Prominent among the twenty is a photographic imager company off Zanker Road in Santa Clara named Foveon, where Mead serves as chairman of the board. Imagers take light from a lens and transform it into electrical signals containing an image. Until early in the new century, nearly all cameras were analog, using film that directly transcribed the image into a visible pictorial pattern. But this is a digital age. In digital you don't make direct chemical analogies of a scene; you translate it into a set of numerical values of the light colors and intensities, which can be processed by computer into the desired picture that you choose to print out.

In September 2003, one month before Mead's stop in Death Valley, digital imagers that converted the picture into a pattern of bits and bytes to be stored on a computer memory exceeded the unit sales of the usual analog film imagers for the first time. Sold in 2003 were close to 35 million digital cameras. Incorporated in cell phones were a rapidly growing additional 10 million digital imagers.

Seven years before, in 1996, Mead founded Foveon to launch an imager for this new era. He devoutly believes that Foveon's imager chip is superior to any other imager in the world. Among many experts in agreement are analysts at several leading photography magazines in Japan and the United States, John Markoff of the *New York Times*, futurist John Dvorak of *PC* magazine, and the photography team at *Consumer Reports*.

Yet here it was seven years after the company's founding, with the market for new imagers exploding, and something at Foveon was way out of phase. Of the nearly 50 million microchip imagers sold in 2003, the Foveon device commanded a share of the market less than one-tenth of 1 percent. Running the company was an interim CEO who planned to return to his previous role as chief financial officer. Richard Lyon, the company's eminent chief scientist, was often on the phone, embroiled in solving technical problems for purchasers of the Sigma camera that used Foveon's imager. Morale was declining. The most prominent board member, Federico Faggin, the Silicon Valley legend who built the first microprocessors at Intel thirty years before, had chosen to take a vacation with his wife in China. The key inventor of the imager, with Mead, was an engineer named Richard Merrill, recently returned from a photography tour in Africa. The key designer of the crucial software systems and imaging algorithms for the device was chief scientist Lyon. He was regaling the industry with learned speeches on the history of photography.

Conducted by Lonergan Richards of Redwood City, a leading Silicon Valley executive search firm, the quest for a new CEO was foundering. With the venture capitalists and company investors on the Foveon board bickering over future strategy, no one knew how to choose among Lonergan's set of candidates, which included major figures from leading semiconductor companies such as Intel and Micron.

Mead, however, is often a contrarian, and he had his reasons to leave the company to its own devices for a spell. In the midst of this critical transition, he chose to turn off his cell phone and set out with his "life partner," Barbara Smith, on a car trip across the country. Said to be hidden deep in the Appalachians in North Carolina were intriguing power-line artifacts that could aid Mead's new efforts to write a history of the creation of the power grid that his father had served for a lifetime.

For ten days, Mead and Barbara had found no relevant relics. But on the eleventh, deep in the mountains where no one had meddled with the equipment, they began to uncover "phenomenal original amplifiers and insulators," the key devices that made the power grid of 1909 work in North Carolina. "This stuff was not covered in any of the histories. No one knew how these systems worked. Everybody had it wrong," Mead said. "To find this stuff is an incredible thrill." Filling up a rental car with the artifacts, they set off for their home in California down Interstate 40 through the Blue Ridge Mountains in Tennessee, down into Texas and New Mexico, and across to Death Valley. After more than two weeks, Mead decided to check his cell phone for messages.

His Verizon service only stored three calls at a time. But one of the messages that somehow got through was a voice mail from a woman named Mildred Porter.

"She alluded to a Fillbond or something," Mead recalls. "I didn't know whether it was a thing or a person." It turned out to be Phil Bond, the undersecretary of Commerce for Technology.

"Has anyone talked to you?" she asked as the cell phone crackled.

"I can't hear you," said Mead, hunched by the gas pumps.

She wanted to know: "Can you do a film for the presentation?"

"What presentation?" Mead asked.

"You don't know!" said Porter. Within a few minutes, Mead managed to learn that he was a recipient of a National Medal of Technology to be awarded by President George W. Bush at the White House.

In the East Room ceremony a month later in early November, Bush would yawn through many of the presentations. But he was concerned about the future of U.S. manufacturing and employment. When he heard of Mead's twenty companies, he exclaimed, "Wow. That's what we need."

Sure. But the president did not know that Mead, standing there in the White House after a fall of travels and historical researches, was on the verge of a failure in his most promising project. Foveon was indeed a company vital to American competitiveness and manufacturing employment. It was targeted to retrieve leadership for the United States in cameras and digital cell-phone imagers, long lost to such Japanese firms as Sony, Fuji, and Canon. But this most promising of American innovations, in the company into which Mead had poured the most energy and creativity, was still drastically out of phase with the market.

With its roots in a research project twenty years before at Caltech in a field called neural networks, developing into a company called Synaptics through the late 1980s and early 1990s, and emerging at Foveon at the turn of the century, Mead's new imager had once seemed likely to be a capstone of his career. Yet U.S. technology had suffered through a devastating crash in the year 2000. Attempting to bring the Foveon imager to market, the company had found the possible U.S. customers, from Kodak to Motorola, in disarray, and the Japanese camera titans such as Canon and Nikon unwilling to rely on a small American start-up for their key imager technology. Amid all the honors and successes, failure at Foveon seemed a distinct possibility as the new century dawned over Death Valley.

Part One

THREE MEN AND A CAMERA

Nobel Laureate Max Delbrück playing backgammon with his son Tobi on the beach at Baja in 1977. Physicist Delbrück pushed Carver Mead into biology, and Tobi became Mead's student and a founder of Foveon. Tobi Delbrück

1

Delbrück Bursts In

arver Mead's path to the Foveon camera began one spring day in 1967 when Max Delbrück burst open for Mead the door between physics and biology. Storming into his Caltech office with a bang and a flurry, Delbrück hurled down a challenge on his desk that lasted the young professor for a lifetime.

A burly man with heavy hornrims and robust humor, Delbrück had gained his doctorate in physics in the early 1930s with quantum theory pioneer Max Born and then had joined patriarch Niels Bohr in Copenhagen. There he had become intrigued with the responses of living things to light, a field then called phototaxis. Defecting to biology, he would win a Nobel in medicine in 1969—two years after his meeting with Mead—for original work conducted at Caltech.

All his life, Delbrück was ready to question the established view, and his questions were seldom solemn. In his Denmark days as a quantum theorist he authored an irreverent satire of

quantum theory—"The Copenhagen Faust"—that was performed for the physicists at Bohr's Institute in 1932 with the
twenty-six-year-old Delbrück himself serving as a top-hatted
master of ceremonies. At the other end of his career, studying
the brain in his book *Mind from Matter?* the sixty-nine-year-old
Delbrück jibed at the neuroscience of his biologist colleagues.
Their efforts to explain the mind as mere material brain, so he
wrote, resembled nothing so much as "Baron Munchausen's
struggle to extract himself from a swamp by pulling on his
own hair."

Now in 1967 Delbrück wanted Mead's opinion on a recent
outpouring of scientific papers comparing the electronics of ion
transfer through nerve channels in the brain with the electrical
behavior of transistors. Thirty-one years old, the lean, sprucely
bearded Mead was already a professor of electrical engineering
at Caltech with a growing reputation as a world-beating expert
on transistor physics.

"These guys are saying that a nerve membrane works like a
transistor. Is this right?" Delbrück asked Mead brusquely. Trans-
ferring electrical signals through membranes in the human nervous system, the nerve channel in biology corresponds on a
superficial level to the conductive channel in a transistor, a tiny
switch or amplifier of electricity invented at Bell Labs in 1947
and used by the millions today in every advanced microchip.
Currents in both seemed to rise exponentially with voltage, and
researchers assumed that the processes were the same.

"I don't know, I'd have to look at the papers," Mead replied
curtly. At the time, Mead did not know who the imperious pro-

fessor was and envisaged papers from biologists with a faint distaste.

"All right," said Delbrück, "here they are." He tossed a formidable pile of printouts in front of Mead.

"I'll look at them," Mead said doubtfully.

During the next week, apprised of the identity of the intruder and rising to the gauntlet hurled on his desk, Mead perused the papers. Quickly warming to the subject, he found himself increasingly dubious of the confident calculations and comparisons between electronic and biological functions. He called Delbrück and commented, "Those papers were interesting, but the model they are using is really garbage."

"In that case," Delbrück responded, "we'll have to find out what's true."

Thus began a long relationship between the two men. Following a summer studying electrical currents in nerve channels at Konstanz in Germany with Delbrück ally Peter Lauger in 1971, Mead designed a special electronic device for plotting the conductance of nerve channels using "black lipid bilayers." These recently invented artificial structures exactly reproduced the physiology of the nerve membrane. Using special catalytic molecules acquired by Delbrück that were known to make membranes conductive, Mead showed that the flow of current across a membrane did not increase exponentially with voltage, but that the number of connections across the membrane did. The brain turned voltage not directly into power but into connectivity. This finding became the prevailing wisdom in the field and deepened Mead's relationship with Delbrück, which also led to a tutorial link with Delbrück's son Tobi at Caltech. After Delbrück's death, Mead became a kind of uncle to Tobi and Tobi became one of the founders of Foveon Corporation.

The elder Delbrück focused Mead on the subject of what Delbrück called *transducer physiology*: all that goes on in a perceptual process between the physical inputs and the first significant output, all the transformations that happen between sense and symbol, between the blinding rush of electromagnetism on the eye and an intelligible image in the mind. Delbrück showed that what we perceive (the image of the world) is radically different from what we receive (the flood of waves on the retina). Vision is far more than photodetection. As MIT's Anya Hurlburt and Tomaso Poggio put it years ago, "Vision is not a sense but an intelligence."

Biologists knew little about these transducer processes beyond rough vectors of connectivity between the retina and the cortex that seemed to assign nearly half of the brain's resources to vision. Mead believed that he had found ways to model some perceptual functions. He assumed that in general brain functions were some fantastic, mostly analog, concoction of currents, chemistry, and timing, with baffling labyrinthine links among them, "high fan-in and fan-out"—lots of connections to and fro.

Although past silicon technology could not yield analog devices with densities remotely comparable to brain tissue, by the early 1980s Mead was moving to create a kind of neural network that rendered "toy" retinas and cochleas out of very large-scale analog-integrated circuits, or analog VLSI. These were chips that used thousands of transistors not as digital number crunchers but as sensors and collectors of real-world inputs. Mead and his team created electronic cochleas that would prove useful in hearing aids and also contrived a series of retina chips.

Although still vastly simpler than the brain, these models offered the glint of new insight into perception. Once you build something, you understand it in a way that you never can through speculation or mere measurement. And once you understand something, grasp its underlying physical foundations, you can build it ever better. This is the virtuous cycle of industrial creation that began with Delbrück's transducer challenge.

The process ultimately led to the creation of what is called a digital imager for a digital camera. The rise of the digital camera is the most sudden and transformative industrial event since the emergence of the personal computer. After the provision of a series of new digital storage devices, such as the compact disc (CD) and the digital video disc (DVD), and after the proliferation around the globe of the wired and wireless Internet, the digital camera opens up the world of electronics to the power of the eye. Anywhere that the network can reach is now a possible site of human vision and vigilance, art and insight. It is the ascendant digital product of the new millennial decade.

Yet nothing reveals the hypertrophy of the digital idea more than the idea, even the phrase, digital camera. There is, after all, really no such thing. The digital camera is an oxymoron because the camera addresses what is chiefly an analog problem: the challenge of creating within a machine a model—an *analog*—of colors, shapes, and textures from the world outside it.

What a so-called digital camera does is to convert analog images from light detectors into three arrays of tiny dots called pixels, or picture elements. In most digital cameras, each pixel bears a numerical value for the intensity of one of the three primary colors—red, green, and blue. Filtering out all but one color at each pixel, the conventional digital imager throws away two-thirds of the light at the outset. Gauging only one of three colors at each pixel, it computes the actual mix of colors on the basis of the value of colors of neighboring pixels. As Carver Mead puts it, the digital camera "guesstimates" the colors.

Carver Mead's obvious, but profound, insight that eventually led to Foveon Corporation was to banish the digital guesswork and use the silicon itself—the substance of a microchip—as a kind of permanent film, like a retina. From the outset, Mead was determined to avoid throwing away information. As Foveon chief scientist, Dick Lyon, explains, they wanted "no guessing at all." From the beginning, they resolved to "measure every color at every pixel." In the Foveon camera, every pixel would register real features of the image rather than digital simulations of it.

At Caltech, long before Foveon was a gleam in his eye, Mead and his team, inspired by Delbrück, learned how to achieve this goal of silicon "film" not by trying to build a computer that would be better than an eye, but by building an eye, actually a retina, in silicon. Embracing the silicon as the physical layer, Mead undertook a deep twenty-year exploration of its analog capabilities. The Foveon camera began not by attempting to transcend analog processes or render them irrelevant, but by exploring both the biology of the human eye and the limitations of digital computers.

Computers can perform instantaneous calculus and create models of short-term weather or store and search the entire contents of the Library of Congress in a disk-drive database. But they cannot see. Even today, recognizing a face glimpsed in a crowd across an airport lobby, two human eyes can do more image processing than all the supercomputers in the world put together. The pursuit of a fully successful camera, therefore, must begin with a study of the human retina and the human brain, and this study, for all the grander claims of brain science, has only just begun.

Now being used in cameras for the first time, the first imager based on a serious study of the human retina and neural system is the Foveon X3. The story of its creation combines themes of neural science and engineering with a tempestuous narrative of business history. From Delbrück and Feynman to Mead and his many students and colleagues, led by Richard Lyon and Richard Merrill, the story brings together some of the paramount figures both in the history of Silicon Valley and in the research community at Caltech. It is a story of minds and brains, and the still mysterious transductive interplay between them, in conflict and creation, in triumph and self-destruction.

Foveon chief scientist Dick Lyon with his high-school yearbook displaying the panoramic product of his third camera, built when he was sixteen. His fourth camera may transform the industry. Dick Lyon

2

The Fourth Camera

As a high-school youth, Dick Lyon showed scant signs of an incipient revolutionary or dasher of icons. He was a nice kid with crisp, smooth features, dancing eyes, and short brown hair brushed neatly to the side. You could see the eyes dance in a photograph he had concocted for the yearbook where his face reflected clearly in the bulge of a shiny faucet in a basin in the physics laboratory. He was head photographer of the yearbook for two years, a good job for a dutiful teenager who respected his elders and the equipment.

In other pictures in his yearbook, nearly all black and white, you could see the eyes of some of the girls dancing around him. The cute blond Leslie, for example, holding the huge slide rule and smiling in the Math Club photo and decorous in many other pictures, definitely was intrigued by Lyon. President of both the Math Club and the Science Club, teacher's pet and polisher, with no signs of a fierce Edisonian scowl or Feynman mischief, Lyon looked twinkly, a bright, well-behaved teenager of the 1950s.

Except it was not the 1950s, but a proxy: the late sixties and early seventies in El Paso, Texas. In his yearbook, the *Roundup*, for his 1970 high-school class, signed by many, girls call him "Einstein" and in a neat, leaning-over-backwards pen, pay humble tribute to his brains and bright future. But his parents knew better and were not especially impressed. Intellectually, they gently imply, he was not up to the standard set by several of his brothers.

"You should ask me about Tom and Jim and Bob . . . yeah and David," says the dad. Why was I focusing on Dick anyway?

"Dick couldn't even spell 'diaphragm' correctly for his Westinghouse Science Prize application," recalls the mom.

"I'm not saying he was slow or anything, and he usually could *spell*. But he really messed up on 'diaphragm.' And his sister, Ellen, is the expert on cameras. Went down to Eastman corporation and made a collection of early Kodaks." But no question, Dick took the most *room* in the house. That wasn't at issue. And there wasn't all that much room to start with.

The Lyons lived in a modest structure with a garage and no basement on a quiet El Paso street, called Fillmore Avenue, where William L. Lyon, Jr., and his writer-editor wife Verna Mae, and their nine children kept the scene mostly under control. Most of the kids would star academically at Austin High School in El Paso, study algebra and precalculus under Mrs. Willie Ingles as Dad did before them, and go on to gain math or science degrees at major universities. A civil engineer, Ellen went to work at Eastman Chemical Corporation and became intrigued with cameras. David, Jim, Tom, and Bill would go to

Princeton. The oldest, David, a mathematician, now does business consulting at Aurora Market Modeling in Manchester, New Hampshire. Bill Lyon III applies advanced math to business projections at the Prediction Company in Santa Fe. Jim also studied mathematics at Princeton and went on to work at Microsoft in Redmond, Washington.

A Unix star at Bell Labs, Tom would become the "eighth badge" at Sun Microsystems (right behind Bill Joy). He helped in adapting the Unix-based operating system that became Solaris. In 1988, he also became famous in Silicon Valley for leading an engineering group in an overnight redesign of the executive offices of Sun CEO, Scott McNealy, and his top assistant into an indoor one-hole golf course, complete with sand trap and water hazard. The can-do Tom was doing what he could to keep the golfer CEO around the Sun headquarters, but finally gave up and defected, to found the IP Router-switch company Ipsilon, which was bought out by Nokia.

Brother Bob, a Cornell man, also became a serious star at Sun, leading the team that created Sun's search software and industry-standard Network File System (NFS), keys to Sun's dominance in networked business computing. When Sun failed to follow his ideas for multiprotocol storage systems, however, he went on to co-found the prominent computer storage software company Legato, now owned by storage titan EMC.

All these kids were well behaved at home. If Dick could not really keep up with his two-years-younger brother, Jim, in math or Tom and Bob in the intricacies of getting rich in software, or David and Bill in abstruse business consulting, maybe that was why he went to Caltech rather than the Ivy League. Maybe that was why he worked so hard, trying to get in on the ground floor, the physical layer, building things and tearing them apart.

One day in 1956, Mr. Lyon returned home from his office at El Paso Power Company and discovered that the four-year-old Dick had entirely dismantled the door lock and was trying to put it back together on the floor. Mr. Lyon was chief engineer at the Power Company, but he found it hard to reassemble the thing so the door would lock again. Mr. Lyon hoped that Dick had learned a lesson. But a year later Dick would be at work dismantling the radio.

At the age of ten, Dick went with his father to his office at El Paso Power, where he showed the young boy the $100,000 Leeds & Northrup computer that controlled the generators at two power plants and transmitted output data back to the central office. All computers have two key aspects—analog and digital. Analog functions connect the computer to the real world of essentially continuous characteristics, such as flows of fluid, radiations of light and sound, temperatures and pressures. The screens, mice, scanners, microphones, and other input and output devices are all basically analog. Digital computing is all numbers, based on binary on-off codes that can be shuffled at a pace of billions of computations per second in digital processors. Mediating between these two worlds—analog flows and digital numbers—are complex devices called analog-to-digital converters (ADCs) and digital-to-analog converters (DACs).

Almost all processing is now done digitally. But for some purposes—chiefly simulations—there are entire computers using analog continuous voltages and currents to represent continuous real-world phenomena. Based on a radar and gun-aiming device that Mr. Lyon had used during World War II, the Leeds & Northrop machine was an analog computer with a complex feedback system. Its purpose was to simulate the flows of high-power electricity through the circuits of the power grid with flows of low-power electricity through the circuits of the computer. The computer would compare the simulated values with desired values and then "feed back" the differences or deltas to control the real power lines. The machine kept the generators and the tie-lines to other utilities balanced and loaded to a level of the "lowest feasible incremental cost."

Lyon had persuaded his boss to buy the Leeds & Northrup computer in 1956, and it had paid for itself in less than a year. As a child, Dick Lyon had been intrigued by the power of this analog machine and its intricate arrangements of internal gears and Selsyn motors. Using these devices today, you could probably make a modern computer or camera the size of the Astrodome. Dick also watched closely for years in the garage as his father plied a metal turning lathe to form model airplane parts, to be assembled into planes that could fly under radio control. All these were physical or analog machines, using real-world materials and functions—inputs and outputs—rather than digital numbers. Watching his father work with these machines, Dick Lyon was learning to be an engineer in touch with the physical foundations of his creed.

Now, however, back in the utility room next to the kitchen, the entire project of raising this boy seemed to be getting out of hand. In there, with the washer-dryer and the water heater, Dick had hung curtains and set up a developing tank as tall as he was and dangled films five feet long with laundry pins. He had spread out boxes of cheap lenses, Kodak E-3 Ektachrome guide-books, cans of black paint, and other—what was it?—*debris*, and now the whole toxic operation was overflowing into the kitchen, where it was getting mixed up with food preparation. On the kitchen table ("Don't worry, Mom") were nine one-gallon A&W Root Beer jugs full of malodorous chemicals. What if one of his siblings should come in from the El Paso heat and take a swig? Now, as a last straw, he was in the garage using Dad's metal lathe to shape Plexiglas into pulleys to attach to the motor he had stolen out of Mrs. Lyon's handheld mixer. Soon they would all have to move out, eat at Pecos Bob's, and convert the whole house into a combined darkroom and laboratory. What did Dick think he was doing?

Mr. Lyon had to admit that his son showed some promise in engineering stuff. Dick had read about Dr. Harold Edgerton's feat of photographing a bullet in flight by triggering the camera with the noise of the gun. He built a strobe light out of equip-ment he found in his dad's garage and a Xenon flash and trigger coil ordered from the Allied radio catalog. Then he set up the apparatus to photograph a Ping-Pong ball as his father hit it. But Mr. Lyon and his son could not coordinate the equipment, including the Ping-Pong paddle, the ball, and the strobe light, well enough in the dark. The ball kept getting lost amid the debris. It was frustrating. Dick decided it would be better any-way—more scientific—to photograph a flying moth.

Delivering the *El Paso Times* and the *Herald Post*, he had saved up enough money by age twelve to buy his first camera, an Olympus Pen-F. He would trigger the shot with a transistor, then still a rarity in household experiments. The moth would fly out of a box, through a light beam, and set off the exposure.

Dad tried to persuade young Dick that making the connections would pose serious problems of *impedance*. Connecting a tiny transistor with the high currents on the wires to his strobe light would resemble linking a drinking straw to a firehose. Dick would need a high impedance source to lower the current to a level that the transistor could accept. But by the time Mr. Lyon came home from the office that evening, Dick had bypassed the impedance issue with a contraption using a light-sensitive photo cell resistor, one of the few vacuum tubes that Lyon ever used. Rather than working with a direct wire connection, it functioned like the actuator on automatic doors. The moth would fly through a light beam focused on the photo cell and make the strobe flash. Mr. Lyon still has several sharp pictures of the moth in flight.

At the high school, though, the girls were not sufficiently captivated by snapshots. Moths in flight, even an ingeniously contrived photo of a water drip in the air, did not impress them. By the time Dick was a sophomore, he had embarked on a more crowd-pleasing strategy. He decided to make really gigantic pictures—pictures that would wow everyone at Austin High. With the goal of becoming head photographer of the yearbook, he set out to contrive panoramic color shots of school scenes and events. Since he could not afford to buy a professional panoramic camera, he would have to build one from scratch. Mr. Lyon had given him some ideas.

In an effort to synchronize the exposure of the film with the rotation of the camera, the young Lyon wrapped 35mm film around a tuna-fish can. Well, it was a beginning. Attached to a tripod, the can could be turned by a hand crank that also moved the lens around the film, exposing it, as the camera scanned the site. This was his dad's idea, and it got him started. But because at each point the image would be moving, it made blurred pictures. Dick recalls, however, that "it was a good idea if it were turned around: By fixing the tuna can and using it to drag the film around a roller to reverse the direction relative to the lens movement and then rotating the whole camera around the fixed can, I got the film movement synchronized with the local image movement behind the lens—for a sharp picture." You may not get the picture exactly, but you may be sure he did.

Anyway, Lyon showed himself to be capable of what might seem an Einsteinian feat of conceiving several objects in El Paso all moving in relation to one another, a piece of film, and the sun. He figured that if the focal length of the lens matched the diameter of the tuna can, a realistic picture could be exposed. Dick took several black-and-white pictures with the contraption. It was his first panoramic camera.

This system never performed to his satisfaction, though, since the negatives—an inch wide and a foot long—were too big to enlarge but not big enough to enable contact prints. He decided to replace the crank with a small electric motor (Mom's mixer motor was at hand). With the mixer blades removed, its speed could be varied and it would not grind, blend, mince, or chop his fingers. He used it simultaneously to rotate the camera and pull the Kodak aerial film across the single-element lens from Edmund Scientific ("a box of cheap lenses went for $5 through the mail"). He constructed a balsa-wood-and-plywood box for the camera. He painted it black. Trying out the device, he initially botched the coordination between the rotation of the camera and the film, yielding tall skinny images. Working in the garage, with the lathe, he contrived Plexiglas pulleys that worked with ball bearings to adjust the movements, so that the one motor could accomplish the two rotation speeds for the film rollers and the camera. Finally the device began producing handsome black-and-white pictures. That was Lyon's major camera number two.

Black and white, however, would no longer do the trick. By 1968, when Dick began the project, most movies and magazines and even family photos were in color. For a yearbook, soon you would need color, he noted, "even in El Paso, where most things are brown and gray." But color greatly complicates photography. Not only do you have to measure the intensity of light of the three primaries, blue, green, and red, as he would fatefully learn later in life, you also have to *matrix* the colors, integrating them for all the intermediate brightnesses and hues. At the time, it was hard enough just to get an accurate-enough exposure (much more demanding than for black-and-white negatives) and then do precise time and temperature control in processing.

Lyon had planned a truly ambitious shot. He wanted a color panorama that would capture the entire quad of the school, all its long sepia buildings, the gray three-story main structure, the gymnasium, the cars parked in the back lot by the tennis courts, the flowers along the lawns, the whole polychromatic shebang in one image. For this, he needed special Kodak Ektachrome film, five and a quarter inches wide and five feet long, designed for aerial color photography.

Here there arose a problem. Nowhere around El Paso could such images be cheaply developed. There was no alternative. Lyon would need to figure out by himself the entire E-3 development process, all the fifteen separate steps, including developer, rinse, hardener, color developer, fix, bleach, rinse, wash, stabilizer, and dry. That meant he would have to take over the utility room for the developer tank and then the kitchen table for the overflow. "I don't think his mom ever forgave him," said Dad in a jocular way. But the results were worth it.

The Austin High School *Roundup* of 1970 contained its first-ever centerfold. Opening up over a full four-page spread, one side showed a black-and-white professional class photo covering 120 degrees. On the other side was a near 360-degree panorama of the quad. Yellow flowers bloomed along the green lawns. Parked in front of the three-story main building was a bright crimson VW bug. In the utility areas was an array of blue and green trucks. Lyon had wanted to have an entire 360-degree cylindrical image, with a green bush appearing at both ends. But that would have taken another page. He settled for the four pager—a unique high-school yearbook displaying its colors like an NBC peacock. Many years later Lyon would bring out the yearbook picture in the course of courting his future wife, Peggy. She was impressed: "Wow! What a nerd!"

Underneath the yearbook panorama was a story about Dick. Describing the prolonged calibration process for the coordinated motion of the motor, the film, and the camera as it panned across the scene, he said, "I'll bet I did fourteen somersaults when I finally got my first good one." He wrote up the process and won third prize in the Trans Pecos Science Fair. Refining the presentation and correcting some of the spelling, he later won first place in the Texas Junior Academy of Sciences, senior division. Of his future plans for the camera, Dick said: "This is my third camera. *Just wait 'til you see my fourth one.*"

BEFORE MAKING ANY fourth camera, Dick Lyon at seventeen went off to Caltech. There he embroiled himself in a series of noncamera projects under his advisor, Carver Mead.

As an undergraduate, Lyon also worked with the world's preeminent scientist of signal processing, John Pierce, spearhead of the Echo and Telstar satellite projects, who came to Caltech after retiring from Bell Labs. Pierce got Lyon a summer job at Bell Labs. There, still only a teenager, Lyon invented new math-intensive digital signal processing (DSP) algorithms for a kind of digital camera that took digitized signals from a satellite, for example, and prepared them to be mapped onto a screen. Still an undergraduate, Lyon became such a DSP prodigy that he taught the subject to undergraduates and faculty members, including Mead.

After graduation from Caltech in 1974, Lyon moved on to Xerox PARC (Palo Alto Research Center), where most of the key components of the personal computer were first put together into practical systems, including the mouse, the iconic user interface, the laser printer, and the Ethernet. Working with Ethernet inventors Bob Metcalfe and David Boggs, Lyons won two patents on an Ethernet timing recovery circuit. In 1980, Lyon invented the optical mouse. Used in various workstations from Xerox and Tektronics, it defined screen locations with a mouse emitting a beam of light detectable on a grid of solid-state photodetectors. It was a kind of device that later became known as a neural network. Simulating the intuitive and associative processing of the brain—with signals that either spurred or inhibited neighboring neurodes—it performed collective computations among clusters of pixels. Thus it could approximate constantly changing and uncertain signals from the user who was moving the mouse by hand.

From Xerox, Lyon went first to Schlumberger's Artificial Intelligence Lab, and then in 1988 to Apple Computer, where he spearheaded the development of the *second* version of the Newton handwriting recognition system (the one that actually worked rather than the one that became haplessly famous in the Doonesbury cartoon for not working, despite much hype from Apple). Through all these research roles, Lyon was piling up patents by the score, most of them related to digital signal processing, pattern recognition, and image processing.

By immersing himself in the Kodak color film process as a boy, however, Lyon had learned the most successful imaging technology ever created. Invented in 1935 as Kodachrome, this multilayered film, using silver halide phosphors, represented the climax of a series of color systems that dominated photography in the hundred years following James Clerk Maxwell's invention of three-shot color and additive color projection. The earlier systems all captured the three primary colors, one at a time—red then green then blue—and then combined them for a projection or print, while the photographer hoped against hope that nothing had moved in the meantime. As the combining process accelerated, the ability to handle moving subjects improved.

A second technique pursued in the first decades of the twentieth century was autochrome. A photographic transparency patented by Auguste and Louis Lumière of France, it used color-sensitive dyed molecules of potato starch, covered with an emulsion spread across a transparent plate like a frame of film, to filter the three colors at once. The random mosaic filter yielded a color transparency when light was reversed into the emulsion through the same random pattern of grains. While this ungainly process of "back propagation" yielded inaccurate colors and modest resolution, the pastel images were pleasing to the eye.

Twentieth-century digital cameras would repeat these essential three-shot and mosaic concepts with three-shot and mosaic charge-coupled device (CCD) systems. With the advance of CCD technology, this essential process of collecting and filtering light intensities first and then computing the colors afterwards has become quick and robust. But the underlying insight—separate registration of the intensities of three primary colors and postexposure mixing and mapping them in a picture—is the same as James Clerk Maxwell's. And the CCD pictures necessarily suffer from the process of first throwing away two-thirds of the light (the other two primary colors) at every pixel at the time of exposure. Digital cameras then recalculate the colors from the hues of neighboring pixels.

As Lyon came to see, this digital camera technology that was taking over in the new millennium was, at the most basic level of capturing colors, a major step backward from Kodachrome. Unlike the one-color CCD, Kodachrome transcended both James Clark Maxwell and mosaic filters by capturing all three colors at once as they penetrated to different vertical levels of the film. By allowing one quick shot on one piece of film, registering all colors and all the light at all locations at once, Kodachrome eliminated the motion and overlay problems of previous systems. Banishing random filters and processing guesswork, Kodachrome would rule color photography for nearly the next fifty years.

Eventually, though, Lyon himself would make vital contributions to a new method of imaging that could eclipse both the CCD digital camera and the Kodachrome system. Laboring through the fifteen steps for developing one color slide, perhaps he let his mind wander to the possibilities of the transistors that intrigued him. Perhaps there began to develop on the subconscious substrate of his mind the idea of a solid-state camera. Like the Ektacrome, it would capture three colors of light at three different levels at every point on the image plane, with no special color filters. With all colors on one chip, it would be fast enough to combine still and motion capabilities and require no developing process at all. All the photographic procedures could occur on the single silicon chip that also captured the image. Advancing at the speed of the computer industry rather than the speed of the camera industry, this breakthrough chip would represent a total revolution in imagers that would achieve both speed and resolution exceeding either Kodachrome slides or Technicolor movies. And it would be hundreds of times cheaper than the equipment of the day.

That was merely a dream. Amid all his distractions, he never got around even to trying to build his promised fourth camera—or the fourth great technology in the history of digital cameras—until he came to Foveon Corporation and rejoined his old Caltech mentor and collaborator, Carver Mead. But in building this new machine—to be named the Foveon imager, after the high-resolution color-sensitive "fovea" in the eye—both Mead and Lyon would need a lot of help from a silicon wizard from Vermont.

Dick Merrill with a Sigma 10 camera containing his handiwork—the Foveon imager that he largely designed and built. He wonders when "Foveon Inside" will become as common a logo as "Intel Inside" is on PCs. According to Carver Mead, Merrill is "the most creative engineer I ever met." Dick Merrill

3

Merrill's View

B *ack to the Future.* "Doc-tor" Emmett Brown at your service—played by Christopher Lloyd—there you have it—
the antic image of Dick Merrill. Wire-rim glasses, long
white coat, electromagnetic blond hair, a bright feral glint in his
skyblue eyes, Merrill will be a familiar figure to all you faithful
time travelers. Just step into this new all-aluminum enclosed
vehicle, with a monochronometer inside to emit just the correct
wavelengths of light, and attach a few score wires to the pins of
your highly analog *flux capacitor* (that's what Steven Spielberg
called it). Then read out the data. "Doc" here will have you winging back into the future in a nanononce.

The reason he can do it, you understand, is that he's ignorant.
"Never underestimate the power of ignorance," Merrill says. He
doesn't mean that he is stark ignorant like an actor who thinks
he can predict global weather over the next hundred years. He
is ignorant and knows he is, and conscious ignorance is a form
of knowledge—is power. In other words, he is an intuitive exper-

imental scientist. That is different from being a highfalutin expert or an academic Ph.D. Merrill is ignorant in the way of a man who went to work first as a carpenter and electrician and only slowly built up to chip design and silicon manufacture. He learned his trade without "being bombarded by professors about how things are for so long that they give you a doctorate for endurance and servility."

"You know," he sums up, "I'm not one of those Caltech guys. . . .

"I might not fit in your story. I wasn't at the top of my class in school. Nowhere near. I can't just do the equations and tell you six reasons why it's not going to work, like Dick Lyon can. I am too ignorant. I will go build the chip anyway—I know how to build chips—and maybe it won't work exactly, but I will find some other useful effect, and it solves the problem."

In other words, he is a genius with silicon.

His problem-solving orientation served him well back in Woodstock, Vermont, where he grew up, in his first job. The son of a prominent local physician, he was oriented toward building things. After graduation from high school in the late 1960s, he became a carpenter. While on the job, though, he found himself serving chiefly as an electrician. At that time in Vermont you did not need any degrees or certificates to wire up houses, and unlike his boss he wasn't afraid of electricity. None of the houses wired by Merrill burned down, to his knowledge, and during the course of his work he figured out how to equip a room so you could turn the lights on or off at either side, folding the wires back and forth three times. It was a real puzzler for a while—as Merrill says, he is none too swift—but he worked it out.

Five years later, after he had made it all the way through math and physics at the University of Vermont in Burlington, he ventured across the Connecticut River to Hanover, New Hampshire, twenty miles northeast of Woodstock, to study electrical engineering at Dartmouth's Thayer School. There the experience with three-way wiring saved him a night of homework. In one of his first classes, the professor stumped most of Merrill's classmates with exactly that problem—how to wire a room so the lights can be switched at either door.

After graduation with a double E (a degree in electrical engineering), Merrill went off to IBM's famous Watson research labs at Yorktown Heights, where he learned the alarming lesson that ignorance can be even more effective when laced with alcohol. Exploring early Metal Oxide Semiconductors (MOS)—the basic microchip technology—he worked for Robert Dennard, legendary inventor of memory chips.

As Merrill heard the story from Dennard, the IBM inventor and his staff went off for a long lunch in April 1964 and began a stint of competitive boozing. Later, stumbling back from the restaurant, they suffered a sudden pang of conscience. They thought it might be good if they accomplished something before leaving for the day. But all of them were too drunk to manage real work. So they decided to do some Really Important Work, worthy of their glorious state of inebriation.

Dennard asked, "What is really important to IBM?" Everyone agreed, memories are important; IBM was then the world's leading producer of memory chips. Memory chips consist of a tiny grid of wires attached to an array of "cells" that store a desired information bit at each point in the grid where the wires cross.

The problem is how to stop the electrical charge representing the bit from draining away through the silicon, which is a sieve to electricity. At the time, each memory cell consisted of six transistors that kept the bits alive by passing them back and forth in what was termed a "flip flop." Together with the wires between them, the six transistors took so much space on the chip that these memories were limited to the low thousands of bits rather than the hundreds of millions or even billions of bits possible today.

"Well, let's invent some better memories," Dennard said.

By the end of a roisterous lunch, the group had arrived at the idea of a single transistor memory cell. It would be based on storing the bit in the form of an electrical charge on a single tiny capacitor, which consists of a conductor sandwiched between two insulators.

"Wouldn't it just leak off?" asked one of the group.

"Yes, I guess the capacitor would flux," Dennard said, "but it could be measured at the end of the line as a sum of the capacitance on the cell and on the wire. You would have to refresh the cell constantly."

"Well, it might work," said one of the team. "That sounds like a good idea, you might call it a dynamic *flux capacitor*. Call the lawyers."

In 1968, IBM patented this one-transistor flux capacitor memory cell, and the rest is history. Bob Noyce, Steven Spielberg, Ted Hoff, Emmett Brown, and the rest of them adopted it in various ways and dynamic random access time-travel became a surefire theme from Silicon Valley to Hollywood, from Richard Feynman to Michael Crichton.

Anyway, that was how Merrill remembered Dennard remembering the invention of the now-prevailing technology for the DRAM, the dynamic random access memory chip. IBM Research offers a more sober tale, starting at a conference on thin film magnetic memories and entailing "many months of work" in an arduously "disciplined innovation process" using the scientific resources of "a unique research environment" to create the "one-transistor dynamic memory cell." At the heart of nearly all the working memory in all the PCs in the world, the capacitor-based single-transistor DRAM cell is one of the key inventions in semiconductor history and according to IBM bravado, "the most abundant man-made object on the planet Earth."

Out of his experience with Dennard, Merrill took a vital lesson. He came to understand that the secret of invention is pattern detection and extension. "There's a lot you can get in this world just by looking for symmetry, looking for patterns," he says.

The pattern of advances in silicon memory was fewer transistors per bit. The zero transistor bit? Sure. IBM had already invented the hard drive in 1956, based on magnetic domains. "Look for a technological trend in one area and apply it to another," Merrill said. Using this technique, Merrill was generating patents for National Semiconductor at a pace of some eight a month when in early 1997 he met Carver Mead at a meeting on CMOS (complementary metal oxide semiconductor) imagers at the National offices on Lawrence Avenue in Sunnyvale. Since the mid-1980s, CMOS has defined the essential structure of nearly all the digital chips in personal computers and other electronic gear.

Merrill met with Carver Mead on several Fridays at National

and at first, he did not even know who Carver was. "He was just this guy doing imagers that were not going to work. They'd seem to work, they gave great demos, but those Caltech guys, they know a lot of stuff, they know much, much more than I do, but they don't know—they can't know—the difference between making something work once in a laboratory and making it repeatedly, in volume, in mass production in a wafer fab. I know that stuff because I have had twenty years of agonizing experience making things by the millions in wafer fabs."

MERRILL'S FREQUENT HABITAT, a wafer fab, is a chip factory, where raw ingots of silicon from beach sand are transformed into microchips through the most complex and rigorous manufacturing process ever conceived by man. Although fabricating the most minuscule devices in all industry, commercial wafer fabs are now mostly too large to compete for real estate in Silicon Valley. Surrounded by moats and metal fences and chemical septic pools, bulbous with huge tanks of deionized water and chemical gasses and buttressed and suspended to absorb the shock of 8.0 Richter scale earthquakes, attended by workers hermetically sealed in white suits, these structures smack of some sleek and angular modern version of a medieval fortress, designed to protect the society's most precious treasures from the outside world. Sequestered in remote parts of the globe, wafer fabs loom on islands such as Kyushu in Japan or bleak desert reaches such as Chandler, Arizona, or even on the wilder edge of Portland, Maine, where National Semiconductor makes its chips.

Arrayed inside these factories is a concatenation of shiny metal machines linked by robotic arms moving quartz boats of silicon wafers—thin gray circular disks usually either eight or twelve inches wide—on and off of carriers. These containers may run on automated tracks that traverse spaces between the equipment like a model amusement park roller coaster or at less automated sites may be borne by fab workers. Surrounding the machines is a controlled environment with mazes of pipes carrying the millions of gallons of deionized water or minute quantities of exotic chemicals into strategic positions. Turbines and filters constantly clean and process the atmosphere in "clean rooms" that are classified by the number of particles smaller than 500 nanometers in diameter in a cubic foot of air. Though entirely invisible to the naked eye, such a particle looms across a microchip as a "boulder." Leading-edge clean rooms at companies like Intel or National Semiconductor are "class ten" or even "class one," meaning that there are between zero and ten such particles, making a microchip factory tens of thousands of times cleaner than a hospital's cleanest surgical facilities.

Using hundreds of millions of dollars worth of the exquisitely calibrated equipment, the fabrication cycle for each silicon wafer lasts six weeks and entails between 700 and 1,000 specific process steps. Transcribing the chip's circuit design onto the silicon surface is a specialized photographic technique called photolithography. It bathes the wafer in near-ultraviolet light— visible wavelengths being between four and eight times larger than the 90-nanometer features that must be inscribed on the chips. The ultraviolet rays shine through reduction lenses in a process that resembles a slide projector with the optics reversed to miniaturize rather than expand the image.

Interspersed with the photolithography steps are hundreds of repetitions of chemical and physical etching, cleaning, ion implanting, diffusing, and "doping" the silicon layers with needed elements to create millions of nanometer-scale devices on every chip. Each wafer holds hundreds of separate chips that are cooked in batches at the appropriate temperature for each chemical reaction or physical deposition and then diced apart after they are probed and tested.

Full of black arts, equipment tweaks, and specialized lore, this wafer-fab process lends its few masters the mystique of a kind of priesthood. Whatever grandiose plans for microchips may emerge from the systems engineers or computer-aided engineering teams at company design centers or from "fabless" microchip firms such as Foveon, it is the fab masters like Merrill who ultimately determine what can be built and how.

Merrill, however, was a rare fab master who also could design chips and invent new devices himself. Merrill thus could innovate not only in chip design but also in chip fabrication, enabling new devices that could not be created by the usual processes. This capability would prove crucial at Foveon Corporation, where the usual industry-standard CMOS processes needed to be adapted to create new forms of analog photodetectors.

Patents had been issued on CMOS imagers as early as 1964. But until the early 1990s, the feature sizes of CMOS transistors were too large to enable an imager with a reasonable number of pixels. For imagers, the industry turned to specialized technology, chiefly charge-coupled devices (CCDs), a custom component partly invented by Carver Mead and his students that took up less space on a chip than transistors did. Like many others in the field, though, Merrill calculated in the mid-1990s that by then microchip progress had advanced enough to enable an imager that uses a cleverly tweaked and controlled version of cheap high-volume CMOS transistors instead of CCDs.

At the time, the entire industry of analog semiconductors was pursuing what was termed "complementary technology." By using both positive and negative electricity—two sources for every measurement—the complementary approach offered immunity to noise and other environmental conditions. Common to both of the complementary signals, these influences cancel out when the difference between the two inputs is calculated.

In 1994, three years before meeting Mead, Merrill decided to create a pixel with complementary output. Exempt from environmental interference, it would allow more stable and accurate imaging. Building this complementary pixel, he discovered that the two channels responded differently to different wavelengths of light. Different wavelengths penetrated different depths into the silicon, making it impossible to make a reliable complementary pixel. But Merrill—listening to the technology—thought this effect might be used in a silicon imager.

With three colors penetrating different depths, a single silicon device might render a full-color image, employing the physical properties of the material. His first tries yielded impossibly murky results, but he thought something might be made of it. "It might not be sharp but at least it would be cheap." Elaborating the manufacturing details, he registered his concept with National's patent lawyers and proceeded on to his next invention. One patent idea down, seven to go for June 1994.

4

The Charged Competition

I n proposing a new silicon image plane for cameras, Carver
Mead, Dick Merrill, and Dick Lyon of Foveon would be
challenging one of the proudest and most profitable
redoubts of Japanese industry. True, like almost every other early
invention in electronics and communications, from the transistor to the laser, the charge-coupled device (CCD) was invented
at Bell Labs, then the giant research arm of AT&T, now serving
its offspring, Lucent and Telcordia. But the Americans went on
to more adaptable memories. The Japanese adopted the CCD
and converted it from a memory cell into an imager, a kind of
light meter that could convert photons into electronic pulses.

In inventing the device in 1969, Bell Labs was seeking what
might be described as a tape player on a chip: a serial memory
with a capacity in megabytes that offered its contents in a continuous stream. At a time when transistors were still relatively
huge, and Intel's first DRAM (dynamic random access memory)
held just 500 bits, a successful megabyte memory chip meant

shrinking each memory domain to as tiny a space as possible. This goal prompted Dennard's pursuit of the one-transistor DRAM cell at IBM. The ideal was not a transistor but a magnetic spot, like the domain on a disk drive. Holding a movable flux of charge in a capacitor, like Dennard's "flux capacitor," the CCD seemed to answer the need for a dense memory device. Because the rectangular grid of CCD capacitors proved to be sensitive to light, the CCD also showed promise as an imager that could efficiently pass on its contents to a memory when the camera's shutter closes.

Leading the quest for the first CCD was Bell Labs' solid-state lab chieftain Jack Morton, who was seeking a silicon alternative to costly magnetic memory for picture phones or answering machines. Responding to Morton's quest were two engineers, then in their thirties, named George Smith and Willard Boyle.

The analog in silicon of a magnetic domain is an electrical charge on a capacitor. Smith and Boyle conceived of a long array of capacitors that passed their charges one to the other, as in a bucket brigade, when dragged along by a voltage stepping along the top.

Patented by Bell Labs, this prototype charge-coupled device was a first step toward the technology that ultimately would supply imagers for most of the world's cameras. However, when Smith and Boyle presented the device to an International Solid State Circuits Conference in 1971, they were surprised to find young Mead student Amr Mohsen presenting a paper he had written with Mead on a sharply improved CCD. Conceived by Mohsen and Mead, the new charge-coupled device used a push voltage to move the charge down the line more swiftly and reliably than a pull voltage could. Although a Bell Labs researcher stood up during the session and declared that it would never work, all current CCDs use the Caltech design. Pushed by a shifting positive voltage, electron charges move down vertical registers or columns to a horizontal buffer. Read out by an on-chip amplifier, the charges are converted into a digital image.

In the great imager confrontation now under way between Foveon and the Japanese, Mead thus can claim at least partial authorship for both of the contenders. But back in 1971, Intel perfected Dennard's DRAM for "working memory" and the erasable programmable read only memory (EPROM), now "flash," for software storage. The CCD went the way of all specialized memory devices unfavored by the onrushing advances of silicon chip technology. Bell Labs soon moved on to other inventions. But when Bell gave up on the CCD, its key developer, Gil Amelio, took over the project. Now famous as a turnaround specialist at Rockwell, National Semiconductor, and Apple Computer, Amelio was then a young researcher working for Smith and Boyle at Bell Labs in Murray Hill, New Jersey. He resolved to turn around the CCD for imaging.

When Amelio moved from Bell Labs to Fairchild Semiconductor, he set out to adapt the device for this new application and made sufficient improvements to be credited as a father of the CCD imager. In the 1970s, Fairchild created a small business in the product for NASA remote sensors on satellites and space probes.

MAKING MANY HUMBLE visits both to Murray Hill and to Silicon Valley from the 1950s through the 1970s, however, were

Sony founders Masaru Ibuka and Kazuo Iwama, together with Makoto Kikuchi, a scientist from Tokyo's Electrochemical Lab and the builder of Japan's first transistor, who became Sony's research chief. As American companies Bell, then Fairchild, then Texas Instruments, and then Rockwell all dropped from the field, Sony wrestled with the technology for some thirty years, gradually eking out a device that could be manufactured by the thousands, with a yield of one or two per wafer. Sony's co-founder, third president, and transistor champion Kazuo Iwama devoted much of his career to pushing the CCD through this unforgiving gauntlet. Embedded in the upper right-hand corner of his gravestone in Kamakura is a CCD chip.

Iwama never lived to see the widespread success of CCDs. But like the transistors pioneered most successfully in Sony handheld radios and like the lasers that were used most widely in Japanese-made CD players, CCDs from Japan finally outperformed those of the American inventors. The Japanese are now manufacturing CCDs by the scores of millions and incorporating them into ingenious camcorders and digital cameras that are a key source of profits for Japanese industry.

In Japan, the CCD saved the solid-state division of Sony Corporation in the 1980s after it failed to keep up in microprocessors and calculators. It enabled the camcorder, made at a rate of some six million a year, to become one of Sony's most profitable products through the 1990s. It became the lowest-noise and highest-performance-image plane for digital photography in the early twenty-first century. Far down the learning curve, the CCD has become one of those established products that has generated an entire industry, supply chain, financial *keiretsu*, and web of manufacturing skills and machines. It benefits from the counterintuitive but remorseless law of business philosopher and pundit Peter Drucker ordaining that no innovation can displace an established system unless it is ten times better. Almost no inventor wants to hear this law, which disgruntles patent holders around the world. But it remains mostly true.

5

Annealing Neurons

At the heart of the science of late 1960s neural networks—computers inspired by a model of the human brain—was a bizarre analogy with the processing of steel. Steel is tempered and strengthened by a technique called annealing—heating it up, cooling it down, heating it up again, cooling it, in a repeated cycle of diminishing amplitudes, sometimes climaxed by plunging the metal into icy water.

Try it some time on your own neural network, if you have a yen for nerves of steel. Sauna, oscillate, sweat, jiggle, shudder, shake and bake, and dive into the wintry bay by the Golden Gate as some people do every year in San Francisco. It will surely refresh you. For a new Silicon Valley start-up—planning utterly to transform both computers and cameras—you are going to have to find a superman or two, men of steel. Perhaps annealing offers a recipe.

What is going on in an annealing process, like the process of developing a film, or even bringing closure to a meeting or purpose to a company, is a quest for a desired condition of the molecules of the material. With a film camera you want an arrangement of silver halide molecules that convey a targeted image. The developing process tips and sloshes the film through a succession of chemicals toward a "program" created when the image is exposed. With an analog computer you want a configuration of electrical energy patterns that conforms to the correct result of the computation, such as the recognition of a face (hi, Carver). With a meeting you want an enduring consensus. With a piece of steel, you want an arrangement of ferric molecules that will not break under pressure or sag softly on a hot day.

A crystalline form—think of ice—arranges the molecular grains of a metal in an aligned structure, riven by shear lines and prone to fracture. Ice resembles a digital system—perfect at every step, and perfectly fragile in the face of a mere bug. Whoops! Emerging from the brine with frost on your eyebrows, you too may feel crunchy and crystalline, ready to shatter into shards. On the other hand, you don't want to be cooked either. A fully heated metal gravitates to a homogeneous array, a malleable clump that does not hold its form. Out of such a glop you will not even be able to extract an image.

What you desire, as a man of steel, is a random distribution of molecules that is free both of the fault lines of a crystal and the ductility of heated metal. To arrive at this point, you need to heat up the molecules, jiggle them around, and shake out the crystalline clumps and shears, without melting them into shapelessness. Your man of steel cannot be a blob. If you are annealing a sword, you need a bendable blade with a sharp cutting edge. When you get what you want, you plunge it into icy water to preserve the result. *Save as*: Deadly-weapon.doc. Or Supermancomic.gif.

Consider it a computational result. If computing does not strike you as a plausible analogy for the processing of a lump of metal, don't worry. That is because schools tend to teach computing as a branch of mathematics, an abstract discipline separate from the physical world. But the physical world, as it changes, is constantly doing computations, transforming the state of its molecules in accord with the algorithms of physical law.

Thus computer scientists see the universe as the ultimate analog computer, processing cosmic cycles of astrophysical, chemical, and geological change toward a graphic result rendered as the landscape, weather, and climate you see through your windows. In that way, computer scientists differ from plumbers, for example, who rarely claim that the universe is merely a Kohler machine, a particularly clever arrangement of cosmic pipes and valves, though such a notion is equally plausible. Carver Mead teaches computer science to biologists and other beginners as a form of plumbing hydraulics.

In annealing, the successive steps of heating up and cooling down a material represent efforts to jiggle and seduce a system toward a desired outcome, shaking out suboptimal fixations or energy disequilibria—errors—on the way. Analogous to heat is height. Both hold potential energy. Imagine a pinball machine with two knobs that enable the player to tilt the tray up and down and back and forth using gravity to maneuver a ball (or several balls) forward toward the goal. Once the ball pops out at the bottom (or pops into a hole), it will not come back. It has arrived at its energy equilibrium. In physics math, such processes are governed by formidable procedures called "Hamiltonians," after the great Irish mathematician William Rowan Hamilton. In 1834 at the age of eighteen, he introduced a "a general method in dynamics, by which the study of the motions of all free systems of attracting or repelling points is reduced to the search and differentiation of one central relation, or characteristic function," which might be gravity, or voltage, or thermal entropy.

Neural networks treat computations as downhill movements toward equilibrium. During the hot phases, the atoms in the material are high up in the topography, full of potential energy, hopping around unpredictably. The solution comes when the system cools off and gravitates to the valleys, the basins, of a low energy equilibrium, the solution set by the computer program or camera image.

But on the way they may come to rest in an upland energy trap, caught in a tree or a high valley, from which they must be shaken free. When a company becomes so ensnared—pursuing some suboptimal goal—it often must be saved by new leadership. Early in the history of the Foveon project, long before there was a Foveon company, long before Dick Merrill and Dick Lyon actively entered the scene, the crucial leadership came from a legendary figure of Silicon Valley named Federico Faggin. It was Faggin who called on Carver Mead to help him with a company Faggin was shaping called Synaptics. Its goal was to exploit the new science of the human brain to create a new kind of microprocessor—the central processing unit in a computer or camera.

Part Two

THE FORGOTTEN
FOUNDER

Federico Faggin at the beginning of his career at Olivetti in 1961 in Borgolombardo, Italy, flanked by technicians helping him test a calculator system he built using some one hundred printed circuit boards. At Intel he would put the same computer power on a single chip. Courtesy of Federico Faggin

6

FF

My any Americans have no idea of who Federico Faggin is, why his arrival at a company would cause a susurrus of comment and expectation in the Valley. However, to the cognoscenti, who knew enough to pronounce his name *Fah-jean*, Federico Faggin was a paragon of integrated circuit design, and the man who contrived the basic microchip technologies that enabled the creation of silicon computers and cameras. If you could see through all the Intel publicity fogs and fabulations—all the sweet smiles and smoke from Regis McKenna PR suits, with their jargon and gentle guidance for journalists and historians—you might understand that Faggin was comparable in his contributions even to the legendary Intel gods, Bob Noyce and Gordon Moore.

Working inside Intel, an Italian immigrant, age twenty-three, with skewed English and few friends in the Valley, Faggin had been the true creator of the microprocessor, the central process-ing unit in nearly every personal computer. This was the product that had made Intel the main company of the California economy, the core holding of every technology investment portfolio, and the crucial physical foundation for the Microsoft empire to the north. The microprocessor also was the product that retrieved the technological edge from Japan in the mid-1980s when the United States' lead in semiconductors—and Intel's profits as well—seemed to be slipping away fast amid a tide of Japanese memory chips. Key to the personal computer revolution and the rise of the Internet, the microprocessor could even be deemed the basis of American commercial power and thus ultimately its military might. Lying at the heart of nearly all major products of U.S. industry, microprocessors inform the cruise control and power brakes in cars, regulate the tuners of television sets, manage the interior environments of tanks, and guide missiles to their targets.

One-tenth of the weight of rival solutions, the original microprocessors thrived in applications requiring absolute minimization of power and size. The first one, Intel's 4004—designed, developed, fabricated, and tested by Faggin—was used in the Apollo spacecraft that took men to the moon.

In those days of large transistors, there was a huge premium on silicon space. You could not waste area on the chip. In the design of the 4004, Faggin adhered faithfully to the rule of minimization. But on the face of the chip, integrated with the silicon circuitry where it could not be removed, he added something extra. Consuming a precious square millimeter or so of area were what appeared to be two malformed additional transistors. Through a microscope, the concerned historian could see that on the border of the chip Faggin had embossed two neat miniature Fs—FF. Faggin's English was still faulty, but he was not shy.

Yes, we all knew, all of us in the know, that it was really Federico, to the extent that one man could be credited, who had *signed* the first microprocessor and was the proximate source of all the bounties of its creation. Even more important, though, in enabling the whole industry to prosper, was Faggin's previous development of a new fabrication method called the *silicon gate process*.

Electronics is a technology of wires and switches: communications links combined with controllable transistor cross-points that can perform logical or sensory functions. In a world of ever more trillions of transistors, the switches become relatively easy. Whether in brains or microprocessors, all computing is ultimately limited by the wires, by the reach and bandwidth of communications. If you cannot integrate the various intermediate results, you cannot finish a computation. Multiplying by the square of the number of nodes or transistors, wires congest the silicon surfaces of chips and the dendritic wetware of the cortex of the brain and the backplanes of computers and the ganglia of eyes and the wiring closets of businesses and the ionic passages of the central nervous system and the under-street circuitry of big cities.

As they increase exponentially with the increase in transistors and processors, wires eventually constrain computation and force *localized* solutions and *distributed* architectures. As Mead remarks, "In the end everything gets choked off by the wires."

That is why, after a few billion years of evolution—and despite several decades of enhancements and upgrades from IBM, Cray, and Intel, despite even the rise of fiber-optic worldwide webs of glass and light—intelligence is still distributed in particular brains and machines, rather than centralized in some transcendent supercomputer in the sky or some pedestal in an air-conditioned computer shrine.

As historic as was Faggin's role in making the first microprocessors, more fundamental in the industry's long-run advance was his contribution to relieving the problem of the wires. Before Faggin, every transistor on a chip had to have a metal wire attached directly to it. This was called a metal gate, an aluminum link to the switching transistor giving it power and connecting it to all the other transistor switches that collectively formed a processor or a memory. Since the transistor was made of silicon and the wire of aluminum, the main problem of semiconductor manufacture was joining the two incompatible substances together in a robust, reliable way.

If your brain used metal gates, your head would weigh a ton, need a direct link to the power grid, and still couldn't recognize Grandma's face in a photograph. The need for a metal gate sharply curbed the industry's ability to put more than a few hundred transistors on a chip. Metal wires melt, drift, leak, and absorb at temperatures far below silicon's thermal limits, often reached during the process of manufacture, which entails multiple cooking steps. Restricted to temperatures below the melting point of metal, many microchip fabrication steps become impossible.

While still at Fairchild Semiconductor Corporation with Noyce, Moore, and Andrew Grove, Faggin developed a way to replace these metal wires with wires made of polysilicon, the amorphous version of the crystalline silicon of the chip. Although scientists at Bell Labs and at Hughes had previously patented some form of silicon gate, they had never made the technology work.

Outside the semiconductor industry, the romance of patents and inventions captivates observers. But within the industry patented inventions are mainly a nuisance that allow others to obstruct your work but do not enable them to consummate it. That is why across the entire industry patents are cross-licensed and shared. Intel's patent portfolio, for example, is shared with Texas Instruments, National Semiconductor, and all the other microchip firms. In general, companies achieve competitive advantage not by patenting ideas, exposing them to the world, but by hiding crucial process steps that are latent in densely wrought and many-layered silicon devices.

In electronics, ideas tend to be relatively easy. They mostly consist of taking functions, such as computers and cameras, already performed on a large scale, and translating them into the small-scale microcosm of microchips. What is hard are not the patents (*patent* derives from the Latin word meaning to "lie open") but the latents (from the Latin word meaning to "lie hidden"): linking thousands and then millions of transistors together in an inscrutably complex chemical and physical weave of layers that reliably executes (and conceals) the idea. What matters is process: making the devices actually function.

Thus the world may exalt Jack Kilby of Texas Instruments for "inventing" the integrated circuit. For his achievement, he won a Nobel Prize and appears on a postage stamp. But the industry saw that Kilby's design, entirely metal gate, with its gold wires arching through air across the top of a chip of germanium, was not manufacturable. The industry knows that before co-founding Intel, Bob Noyce invented the real silicon integrated circuit while at Fairchild Semiconductor and with Gordon Moore, Jean Hoerni, Faggin, and others made it work.

In developing the silicon gate, Faggin also contrived an exquisitely accurate method for laying down these polysilicon wires on the chip substrate and connecting them to the transistor so they aligned themselves in exactly the right place. It was a *self-aligned* silicon gate.

Allowing the creation of transistors made entirely of various forms of silicon—sand—the Faggin breakthrough of silicon gates gave the technology at least a temporary reprieve from the tyranny of wires. Most of the chip could be completed before you had to worry about the metal and its melting point. After Faggin, wires and switches could be made of the same essential material.

Although no one recognized it at the time, the silicon gate was the first critical step toward a totally new paradigm: a global network of wires and switches dominantly wrought of silicon and silica, which are various permutations of sand. The substrate of chips would be opaque silicon, and the network would be transparent silicon (fiber-optic glass). Ultimately, nearly all information technology, from networks and cell phones to computers and cameras, would consist of various forms and aggregations of silicon gates.

Enabling this all-silicon infrastructure will be all-optical long-distance systems, where the wires evanesce into mere wavelengths on fiber threads and the switches evolve into passive optical waveguides like prisms. This consummation of Faggin's silicon gate—his first step for mankind—is still under construction in 2005 and skeptics believe it will never be built, though a company called Corvis has already run such a network for its subsidiary Broadwing. Jerome Wiesner and the other science advisers of President John Kennedy, remember, all believed that the Apollo project was impossible as well.

By sending the signal from origin to destination entirely on wings of light, the all-optical network obviates the electronic conversions and regenerations, synchronizations and retransmissions that raise cost and complication in existing networks. Vastly simplifying and accelerating all communications, optics can enhance the audio and video resolution of every film, teleconference, medical image, game, or cultural event that plays across the Internet.

Digital computers and cameras and cell phones are already mostly silicon. An electronic camera, in particular, would be almost impossible with metal gates, since metal cannot detect colors of light. Eventually, silica fiber optics will replace all the copper cages and metal harnesses of existing telephone systems, and the network will be silicon too and will transmit pictures as readily as it now handles voices. Faggin's concept will be everywhere. With the wires and switches, computers and cameras, all made of the same essential substances, they might ultimately work at the same speeds, allowing the distribution of computing and vision across an entire worldwide web of sand and light.

7

Beyond the Silicon Gate

Back in 1969, while Neil Armstrong capered on the lunar surface, silicon cameras and all-optical networks lay in the long and still-embattled future. At that time, as Robert Noyce and Gordon Moore left Fairchild Semiconductor to form Intel, Federico Faggin faced more immediate problems. Hobbled by restrictions on his visa, the young Italian stayed behind at Fairchild, while Sherman Fairchild and the company management back in Long Island tried to figure out what to do with their depleted Silicon Valley subsidiary. Faggin was not at the forefront of their plans. Meanwhile, the U.S. government did not want the young Italian with his physics doctorate from the University of Padua to take any jobs from Americans without due process of bureaucracy. His experience in Italy had begun with a stint with Olivetti at age nineteen, when he had provided the former typewriter company with a design for what was then seen as a "small" computer (well, it had only a hundred printed circuit boards, deemed heroically few at the time). Think how many jobs for low-income Americans that kind of mischief could cost.

So Faggin had to stay put at Fairchild. Through the Silicon Valley rumor mill, he heard that Intel was experimenting with silicon gates. "If they are," said his boss at Fairchild, "we'll sue them." At the time, Faggin did not know about American lawyers and was startled by this idea. He just wanted to work on his technology, and Fairchild was letting it drift. Each day, so it seemed, another key man would leave the company. Nearly last to depart was the young Hungarian chemist Andy Grove, who had at first resisted moving to Intel out of suspicions toward all this frothy talk of compensation in shares. Faggin wondered why someone from Intel didn't call him. They could help him with the visa, and he could help with silicon-gate processes. He still knew many useful secrets. And he would be more than happy to take shares. But he had to stay back. Bearing their first child, his wife, Alvia, became restive. They had few friends in the Valley. Perhaps Federico should return to Italy.

It took some six months to work out the visa details. Finally Faggin called up Les Vadasz, his former Fairchild superior, then at Intel, and asked to come to Intel to work on silicon gates. Vadasz thought for a moment and said "Yes." He had an idea for a mysterious new project. It turned out that this new silicon-gate project was a complex device that Intel had contracted to create for a Japanese calculator company, named Busicom, and that could not be readily built without Faggin's intimate knowledge of polysilicon processes. Crucial were the so-called *buried layers* or "doped" silicon contacts that made the connections from Faggin's silicon wires to the transistors below.

The silicon-gate process enabled Intel to put some 2,400 transistors on a chip, enough to build an entire central processing unit on a single sliver of silicon. A "computer-on-a-chip," this was the microprocessor, a feat long targeted by various visionaries in the industry but only vaguely outlined at the time and not economically manufacturable without Faggin's technology.

The day after Vadasz hired Faggin to build the new device, Masatoshi Shima showed up at Intel from Busicom in Japan to check out their microprocessor project. In December 1969, Shima had finally persuaded his company, which had been cluelessly seeking a calculator chip set with ten separate designs, to accept Intel's unorthodox one-chip concept. But by April 1970, when Shima arrived, the microprocessor remained a low priority item at Intel, which still fancied itself a memory company. Since Shima had signed off on the project in December, it had already slipped five months behind schedule.

As Shima put it angrily when Faggin showed him the specs, "I already see those. Where is the logic design? Where are the circuits? There is nothing here. This is not a device. It is only *idea*. I came all way over here to check. There is nothing to check." Shima was furious that Intel had made no progress on the project since he had left. Faggin had to persuade Shima to stay and help him make it into a real microprocessor. With a hand crippled in a boyhood rocket experiment, Shima's capabilities were doubted in corporate circles in Japan, and he was intrigued by the opportunity to come to the United States. He stayed for twenty years, until rehired by Intel to start a research center at Tsukuba in Japan.

From the silicon-gate concept later evolved a "floating gate."

Crucial in memory chips that do not lose their contents when the power goes out, a floating gate is an insulated island within the silicon device treated to accept electronic charge and hold it. Faggin inadvertently discovered floating gates for himself in the first rendition of the microprocessor when "the big day came in the end of December 1970" and he could test the wafer at last. Chips are made in batches on wafers, each containing a large number of actual chips. It was after 6 P.M. on that December evening after Christmas, and most of the other engineers had left for the day. Alone in the lab in Mountain View, Faggin was measuring the electrical behavior of the device through an oscilloscope, the ubiquitous box with a little blue or green screen that provides a window for the engineer into the invisible electronic world on the chip. He attached the delicate probes of the tester to a die (an unseparated chip on a wafer containing many dies).

As he wrote later, "I pushed the start test button and . . . nothing. I mean nothing, not even a wiggle anywhere on the oscilloscope. I told myself, it's a bad die, let me try another one: Same story . . . I changed the wafer and repeated the process. Same result. By now I was profusely sweating, thinking: How could I have screwed up so bad? I continued to test more dies and more wafers. No life. After 20 minutes of agony I finally decided to take a look under the microscope. Something must be wrong! It didn't take long to find out that [Faggin's unorthodox] buried-layer masking step was left out of the process [by Intel's wafer fab team] . . . Most of the gates were floating!"

Insulated from any electrical connection, a floating gate is useless as the control element in a transistor, but would prove useful as a memory cell that could hold an electrical charge for a period measured not in the mere milliseconds of a capacitor but in years or even decades. Also in Mountain View at the time, an Israeli named Dov Frohman was independently perfecting floating gates as a memory element for erasable programmable read only memories (EPROMs). When on November 15, 1971, Intel launched "a new era in integrated electronics," it announced four chips: for calculations, Faggin's microprocessor; for software storage, Frohman's EPROM; for working storage, a dynamic random-access memory; and to interface between the processor and memory, a small register chip. In sum, Intel introduced all the key components for a personal computer and all of them used silicon gates.

The concept of floating gates especially intrigued Faggin, who saw it as an extension of his own silicon-gate concept. After the EPROM, the floating gate enabled a series of nonvolatile memories—memory chips that kept their contents when the power went off. Based on the floating-gate concept is today's "flash" memory, holding programs and data on your cell phone, start-up data in your computer, and images in your digital camera.

Faggin was a vital catalyst for all these developments. And yet, in 1986, some fifteen years later, he was still in Silicon Valley, still building chips, and almost entirely unacknowledged by journalists and historians in the industry. Only the experts knew that personal computers had Faggin's work inside. The key reason for Faggin's eclipse was his departure from Intel in 1978 with his collaborator the *"nobushi"* (cantankerous) genius Shima to start a new company. At a time when the company's lawyers were prowling the globe to protect Intel's precious intellectual property and to deter similarly pregnant defections from Intel itself, it would not do to let the world know the story of Faggin and the silicon gate. So the man who had transferred the key intellectual property of Fairchild to Intel in his spruce and volatile Paduan pate was written out of Intel histories as some kind of embarrassment.

Faggin had many reasons to leave. Intel was too large, too preoccupied with the memory market, too concentrated in ownership in the founding group, too oriented toward a hagiography of Noyce and Moore to celebrate and reward the accomplishments of Faggin. In addition, Andy Grove had instituted a sign-in sheet that has become infamous at Intel. "If you arrived at the office after eight in the morning, you had to sign in." Clearly, it was time to go. Faggin was willing to sign in his initials on silicon (FF), provided it was a device of epochal importance, but this was a bridge too far. He felt "subjugated."

As a practical matter, though, even in Silicon Valley, you cannot just spin out and start a new company without support from banks and venture capitalists. For Faggin, the vital factor was the opportunity. Intel had yet to focus fully on the microprocessor. Faggin and Shima formed Zilog Corporation to do the microprocessor right! At Zilog, Faggin led the design of the Z-80, a new microprocessor, which was decisively superior to the Intel processor and would enjoy a longer life span embedded in low-rent electronics products. However, the central role of the microprocessor in a computer architecture is to define its "instruction set," the portfolio of things that it can directly do, such as add, subtract, or fetch from memory.

Directly addressed by every computer's software operating system (OS)—such as Windows or Linux—these instructions vary subtly between different microprocessors, even very similar ones like the Intel 8088 and the Z-80. The subtle variations among instruction sets pass on as a kind of DNA into the software operating systems that run the basic operations of a computer, and then from the OS into all the applications such as Word and PhotoShop that use that OS.

Faggin set the Z-80 to execute Design Research DOS instructions, thus obviating the need to pay Microsoft fees. Adopting the Z-80 was Tandy Radio Shack for the "Trash 80" home computer. Adopting the 8088 from Intel was IBM for its personal computer. As a microcontroller embedded in everything from automobiles to copiers, the Z-80 eventually sold in the billions for single-digit dollars. In the long run, however, going behind the back of Bill Gates and his DOS did not turn out to be wise. In the exalted realm of computer central-processing units where margins lurked near 50 percent and chips sold for hundreds of times more, Intel would crush the Z-80 entirely. Crush Faggin.

In those benighted days before the trial lawyers banned all pithy or revealing corporate communications, before casual e-mails came burdened with seventeen lines of disclaimers at the bottom, and before the Justice Department focused its big guns on various forms of managerial faux pas, Intel used that term "crush" a lot to convey its goals in relation to its competitors. Its much-acclaimed campaign against Motorola's 68000 microprocessor was called Operation Crush. Bill Gates noticed. He liked to crush rivals, too. In this slam dance of industrial elephants, Faggin was lucky to get out alive. He would not even get rich, let alone famous.

IT WAS FAGGIN who launched the play, but he and Shima became Rosencrantz and Guildenstern in Intel's version of *Hamlet*. History is written by the winners. Intel is a great company, and among the privileges of greatness is not only to make history but to rewrite it. The company-certified inventor of the microprocessor would be Ted Hoff, the nice owlish man from Rochester, New York, who had conceived the general architecture of the chip. It was not an exceptional architecture at all, based as it was on Digital Equipment Corporation's minicomputer, the PDP-8, and not really a new idea. Expressive of what the industry called "spaghetti design," the PDP-8 devoted most of its space to metal wires between the components on the printed circuit board. Put those wires on a modern microprocessor, without Faggin's silicon gates, and the thing would sprawl over several blocks of Santa Clara.

Hoff was a smart and creative man who proposed the obvious integrated solution for a calculator chip. He stayed around and didn't make waves, and mused modestly about chips for speech recognition. But Intel was not interested. It had become the microprocessor company, period, and more ideas were supererogatory. Hoff had had his certified idea and he was Intel's man. He would win the kudos, until Intel got bored with Hoff as well and he went off to become a fellow at a research institute.

However, the feisty Federico—FF—was not the "fellow" type. In a Silicon Valley macho moment, he observed: "You aren't really a man until you start a company." If he had come to wive it wisely in Padua and had moved to jive it wealthily in Santa Clara, he had ended up with relatively little money, and a "pushy" wife, so they said at Intel, who thought her husband should get credit for what he had done. Imagine that. Forget Faggin—*Faggin outside*—was the Intel consensus.

Largely crush-proof, however, Faggin was difficult to forget. And Alvia, a technical writer, was still pushing to make the world grasp her husband's role in the first microprocessor. She would ultimately prevail, but the world of technology was slow in personal matters, and Intel-oriented. In 1986, Faggin thought he might make history yet again, find yet another chance for fame and fortune and enduring achievement, by founding yet another company resolved to replace his first invention with a new one, a company poised to take advantage of the latest innovations in another computer model, the neural network.

8

Tobermory

Like many smart engineers in the industry, Federico Faggin deemed the prevailing microprocessor designs—even his own—as cumbersome, inflexible, and too dependent on software for interfaces to the outside world. Based on the architecture credited to the great Hungarian genius John von Neumann, all these microprocessors followed a serial regime, step-by-step, getting instructions and data from memory, processing the operands one at a time, and sending the results back to memory. "Step 'n' Fetchit" was the drill. Von Neumann machines were so dominant that any other design was termed a *non-von*.

Although von Neumann computers were efficient at performing routine mathematical functions and simple step-wise algorithms for spreadsheets and word processors, they bogged down on a variety of more complex problems. Not only did they fail to meet the famous supercomputer grand challenges of chaos and nonlinearity, fluid flow and phase changes, weather modeling and molecular chemistry, they also failed at pattern recognition, vision, and haptics—all functions that might be summed up as simulating human sense and sensory input.

Daniel Hillis was the designer of several formidable "non-von" "Thinking Machines" employing a massively parallel design called cellular automata. Although based on yet another of von Neumann's ideas, computers optimized for cellular automata were deemed "non-von" by an industry that could not quite come to terms with the polymathic genius of von Neumann. Hillis described the problem of von Neumann's original step-by-step architecture as "the paradox of common sense," or why sense is not common in computer science. Among humans, common sense springs from lots of knowledge about the details of the environment. In general, the more humans learn, the better they function. The more they know, the more they can sense and see. But in a computer, it is the opposite. The more it learns, the dumber it gets. The more knowledge that is put into a von Neumann computer, the bigger and more crowded its memory and the slower it functions. That is why your Google search engine runs not on one huge computer and one centralized data base but on one hundred and twelve thousand networked small computers, using Pentiums, the great-grand-kin of Faggin's microprocessor design.

Hillis explained the problem in his book, *The Connection Machine*: "As we build bigger machines with more silicon, or equivalently, as we squeeze more transistors into each unit of area, the machines have a larger ratio of memory to processing power and are consequently even less efficient. This inefficiency remains no matter how fast we make the processor, because the length of the computation becomes dominated by the time required to move data between processor and memory."

This time sump is called the von Neumann bottleneck. To overcome it was the grail of much computer science of the day. Emerging in the universities was a new movement led by Hillis, David McClelland, William Dally, Chuck Seitz, Steve Colley, and many others who advocated removing the von Neumann bottleneck by multiplying the processors and coupling memory to each one, distributed through the machine. Known by many names, the concept was massively parallel processing. Based in part on models of human brain functions, the new designs would eschew the step-by-step regime and adopt parallel methods that could simultaneously process scores or even thousands of bit-streams.

One persistent line of research focused on what were called neural networks, which were computers based on a primitive idea of how billions of neurons might work together in the human brain. In the early 1980s, for all their popularity as an academic pursuit, neural networks remained an obscure backwater in the computer industry. In the late 1960s, a one-time enthusiast, MIT computer scientist Marvin Minsky, with colleague Seymour Papert, had shown that neural networks could not perform logical operations critical for serious computing. At the time, the most resourceful advocate of neural nets was Frank Rosenblatt of Cornell, inventor of the "perceptron," an early form of neural network optimized for imaging.

Today, Rosenblatt's device, named Tobermory after a fictional cat that could understand human conversations, sits in the Smithsonian Institution in Washington, next to von Neumann's first computer model, as if comparable inventions. But Rosenblatt never saw this vindication. He died in a somewhat mysterious boating accident on Chesapeake Bay after apparently losing a debate to Minsky. Rosenblatt's most fervent disciples believed it was a heinous crime. "I accuse: *Dr. Minsky on the bay, with an algorithm.*"

Minsky showed that while any digital computer can mimic the series of additions and multiplications of a neural network, Rosenblatt's simple one-layer perceptrons could not perform key digital computer functions, called Boolean logic, necessary for the execution of digital computer programs. Since the digital computer could do any calculation the Tobermory could do, but Tobermory could not perform key digital functions, Minsky and others dismissed the utility of Rosenblatt's machine. As a result, the perceptron idea lay in limbo for two decades.

By the 1980s, however, the flaws of the von Neumann design led to a new look for alternatives. Digital computers might be Universal Turing Machines (named after Alan Turing, the British genius who conceived them during World War II while breaking the German Enigma code). A digital computer might simulate anything in the cosmos that can be reduced to numbers. But digital computers could not interact with the real world. They were deaf, dumb, blind, and insensate. "Dumber than an airport urinal," as Nicholas Negroponte puts it, since the urinal at least knows that you are there. Computers may aim to be "general problem solvers" but they could never solve the problems of driving a car, emulating a retina, or taking a photograph. After decades laboring in the Artificial Intelligence Lab at MIT, Minsky, himself, concluded that the most challenging form of intelligence was not the manipulation of numbers, whether in high-school arithmetic or advanced calculus, but the perception of the real world—all the seeing, hearing, touching, and motor skills that are learned in the first year of life. Once the image or the input is converted to numbers, the problem has basically been solved. It becomes SMOP (simply a matter of programming). Neural networks were designed to address these problems of pattern recognition that the digital computer could not do at all. That neural nets like Tobermory might be slow Turing machines seemed irrelevant.

But to push neural nets to the point that they could create an image or register a touch or recognize a face or take a picture would require a series of innovative jolts imparted by rivalrous professors at Caltech.

9

The Hopfield Net

In its 1980s revival at California Institute of Technology, neural network research reached a moment of revelation at an evening meeting of the American Science Association. There a Caltech physics professor named John Hopfield introduced the Hopfield net, a model for a neural network based on an abstracted cartoon of the functions of neurons in the brain. These neurons had none of the features of wetware, no DNA or complex biochemistry. But the mathematical rules that governed their behavior and their massive connectivity—fan-in, fan-out in electronic terms—seemed crudely congruent with the way the brain functions in seeing, hearing, feeling, and recognizing patterns.

Comparing his computational model to the digital model, he offered the analogy of two different approaches for a committee to make decisions. "In a digital computer-style committee the members vote yes or no in sequence; each member knows about only a few preceding votes and cannot change a vote once it is cast. In contrast, in a collective-decision committee the members vote together and can express a range of opinions; the members know about all the other votes and can change their opinions. The committee generates a collective decision, or what might be called the sense of the meeting."

A meeting that gravitates toward a consensus—an analog meeting where everyone buys in to the decision—is likely to produce a more stable and robust outcome than a binary up-down vote from a digital meeting. Supposedly run by consensus, Japanese companies do not spin out a lot of competitive companies. Advocates of neural computing hoped to create devices that were robust in the face of errors, bugs, or fuzzy inputs from the real world. Such a computer could conceivably become a camera, or an eye.

What made Hopfield's vision irresistible to many brain scientists, physicists, and entrepreneurs alike was its mathematical foundation in the natural physics of spin glass. These were arrays of magnetized glass molecules (silica) that could be heated into an excited flux, with each molecular grain "frustrated," or poised between two binary states by the magnetic forces impinging on it from neighboring grains. Small effects could tip a polarization one way or another, triggering a cascade of change to neighboring grains. Governed by the laws of least action and lowest energy, the synthetic neural network would gravitate as much as possible to its lowest energy state, signifying a consensus—all argument subdued—which represented a solution to the targeted problem. Because a spin glass was a natural object, researchers thought it might offer clues to the mysteries of brains, eyes, ears, and other natural objects.

One way to simulate such a network is to interconnect densely an array of simple processor elements, usually termed neurons but better named "neurodes" to save the biological name for real neurons. Like cellular automata, neurodes sum up the inputs of all contiguous processors. This is a "high fan-in and fan-out" arrangement with lots of connections both in and out. Responding to the collection of inputs with an output action that in turn becomes an input for neighboring processors, the system over time arrives at an optimal point: the solution. By making the topology—pattern of energy peaks and basins—programmable at each processor through a pattern of weights on the neurodes, the neural network designer can create a general-purpose computer without a memory bottleneck.

Each configuration of the entire machine could represent a particular pattern of sounds in a speech recognizer, or of financial data in a securities analyzer, or of cranial shapes in a face recognizer. In theory, then, and in practice soon after, such devices could identify fingerprints, buying opportunities, bacteria, credit-card fraud, power-plant perils, or terrorist maneuvers. The network may be trained by showing it a desired pattern of inputs, which result in a particular weight for each neurode. The pattern of weights is the program for the device. Thus the "common sense" of the machine was not concentrated in some centralized memory but diffused through the entire network, like the information in a hologram.

Faggin had been tracking all these developments as he developed his new company, which he would call Synaptics. His first insight was that a programmable neural network could become a preferred form of processor for all pattern-matching functions, such as hearing, imaging, touch, and other computer inputs. Since every computer or cell phone or camera would spend much of its time recognizing patterns of various kinds, a general-purpose pattern recognizer could find a market that might be comparable in size to the market for von Neuman microprocessors like the one Faggin had created at Intel some fifteen years before.

Faggin's further insight was that his "floating gates" could function as the memory element for the neurode weights. He envisaged a programmable neural network based on floating gates that could be trained to perform any pattern-recognizing role. "Guess, measure the error, adjust the answer, and feed it back" is the basic routine of neural networks: an iterative process that step-by-step approaches the answer to problems, such as: "Is that Bin Laden's face or a bagel?" or "What is that object in the Tumi bag?" that cannot be computed by ordinary machines.

Once again, as in the case of the original microprocessor, intellectuals thought they knew what a neural network was, but no one could build an effective and marketable device. Like most researchers who explored the field, Faggin found himself gravitating toward the work of Mead, then building his large-scale neural networks on microchips. Even though his neural networks were only roughly related to the models of Hopfield and McClelland and the other pioneers who had originally attracted Faggin, Mead was pursuing a quest for practical devices rather than for exalted but elusive theory. He was beginning to transform his Caltech lab from a center of leading-edge digital devices and design tools into an arena of what he called Analog VLSI.

Mead and his students began converting ordinary digital VLSI chip substrates such as are used in Faggin's microprocessors, made by the billions in semiconductor factories around the globe, into analog circuits that could crudely reproduce brain functions. Because he was using the most common semiconductor processes, his devices could be cheap, containing thousands of transistors. Because he used these transistors in analog form—not switching on and off like a digital device but operating continuously like an AM radio tuner—he could make an analog sensor with as many transistors as a digital microprocessor has, eventually millions. To tap these resources for his new company, Faggin would have to come to terms with Carverland.

Part Three

THE CAT AND THE CAMERA

10

Carverland

eginning in 1983, the center of Carver Mead's world—
his students called it Carverland—was his laboratory
above the janitorial warehouse and machine shop at Caltech. Originally classed as "second-class space," this second-
story facility filled up with equipment and avid students and
became a hive of creative activity on the campus. To get a
glimpse of some of the players, let us set up a pretend neural
network at LAX and weight its synapses for brilliant nerdy high-
school males headed for Pasadena for the fall semester. Jack up
the synapses for acne, ponytails, ham radios, plastic pocket pro-
tectors, model-airplane kits, copies of *Gödel, Escher, Bach,* and
advanced graphic calculators. (Let that big girl with granny
glasses and denim overalls and the comic books under her arm
pass right through, shunted by the neural network into the art-
school queue.)

One way or another, the synaptic machine might catch many of
the rest—including, for the purposes of this tale, David Gillespie,

Tobi Delbrück, Tim Allen, Adam Greenblatt, Tom Tucker, Glenn Gribble, David Feinstein, John Platt, and even a few older participants—instructors—such as Dick Lyon, who wore a ponytail and fit the mold. In 1984, Lyon had joined the Schlumberger Artificial Intelligence Lab in Mountain View after his stint at Xerox PARC. From these perches in Silicon Valley, he continued to commute regularly down to Carverland in Pasadena to guide each new generation, work with Carver on difficult technical problems, and tutor exceptional students.

Now that our neural net has caught them, let's meet our specimens. Near the entrance to Mead's lab throughout most of the 1980s was a fuzzy-faced blond boy also with a ponytail, leaning toward the large screen of an HP Chipmunk workstation. When he was introduced ("This is Dave Gillespie"), he would shuffle and shift on his feet, look down and away, and back at the screen. He really had to get back to his project. A Caltech sophomore, he was ginning up a design tool for timing parameters on digital circuits that Carver considered "pretty neat." And "Carver had the coolest computers," so the young undergrad began to hang around the lab. Soon he was there day and night.

"I managed to horn in on all the coolest professors," he says. He ended up as a teaching assistant in Richard Feynman's course, "The Physics of Computation." He also twice led Caltech to victory in national Association of Computing Machines (ACM) programming contests and then became coach. Taking the Hopfield course in neural nets, he would not only do the homework but also code computer programs to perform the homework automatically. Even before graduating, he started actually giving the freshman course in computer science. "Except for Carver, most of the top professors steered clear of freshmen. I found them great. I liked turning them on. I liked explaining the stuff."

Within an important group of other scholars such as Glenn Gribble, Telle Whitney, and John Lazzaro, who supplied the lab with design tools and software, Gillespie became a fixture in Carverland. In an extraordinary feat, he contrived to spend a full decade at Caltech, including six years in graduate school. It was not until 1991 that he turned off onto Interstate Route 5 and drove up the coast to Zanker Road in Santa Clara, where he joined another lab that looked pretty much the same, with the same faces and much of the same equipment. The company was Synaptics, almost five years old at the time, the first corporate vessel of the imager project that would end as the Foveon X3.

Often working with David Gillespie at Carver's lab in the 1980s was Tobi Delbrück. Max's son, a large, shambling man, unassuming and practical, Tobi was perhaps the most adept engineer in the lab, ingenious at contriving workable breadboards (test boards with an array of working electronic devices on them), incorporating the various circuits and devices created by Mead and the other students. He frequently collaborated on imagers with colleagues. Later contriving a stream of retina chips himself—for camera imagers, door openers, check readers, and autofocus detectors—he built many of the imagers used at Synaptics. Nonetheless, industrial engineering was never his true calling. Like his laureate father, he was called to basic research on the frontiers of science.

Sharing an office next to the Caltech lab were John Platt and David Feinstein. Even at Caltech, where "beautiful minds" abound, these paragons of mathematics were a rare and coveted resource. Although Platt was Mead's graduate advisee, he shared his services with John Hopfield; Feinstein worked both with Hopfield and with Richard Feynman while writing a Ph.D. thesis with Mead.

With curly black hair and a boyish look that had not left him twenty years later, John Platt exhausted high school by age fourteen. He passed through the computer science program at Long Beach State in three years, and came to Pasadena for graduate studies. When he arrived at age eighteen in 1982, Carver's lab was still in cramped quarters in Booth Hall, where the only analog project was a circuit of sufficiently low power to be run on incident light. Moving in 1983 to the new Carverland—the larger space over the janitor's machine shop—Platt began a fruitful collaboration with Mead on the use of timing dynamics in neural models, delays and buffers that give them the analog counterpart of short-term memory in digital systems. Mead was sure that crucial to the brain's computational process was the use of time. Rather than marching to the beat of an abstract clock, the brain uses the time of arrival of an input as a source of information and its relationship to other timing events as a mode of computation. For example, the brain apparently distinguishes a word from a chaotic flow of sounds by the appearance of several phonemes enjambed back-to-back.

Presenting a prototype system to Carver, Platt in his first year declared that his scheme was asynchronous (without a regular clock cycle) and thus would be immune to variations in the speed of components. Mead challenged him. "Then it shouldn't matter if you take out this capacitor?" he said, pointing to a small circular device that stored or delayed electrical charge on the prototype board.

Platt hedged. "Well, maybe." Platt had a mathematical theory but had not tested it. He took a deep breath and yanked the capacitor off the board while the circuit was running. It continued to work, meaning that the circuit was truly asynchronous and thus did not depend on a particular cadence of timing and delays.

Carver burst into a smile and slapped him on the back. "That's terrific!" he said, delighted as usual with every show of achievement by his students. Platt's work on the use of time as a mode of computing eventually led to collaboration with Mead and Dick Lyon in the creation of an ingenious model of the human cochlea, which imitated the human ear by separating sound frequencies according to the time they take to pass down the auditory channel. After getting his Ph.D. under Mead in 1985, Platt joined Lyon as an intern at Schlumberger.

In pure intellectual fireworks, though, Platt more than met his match in his office mate David Feinstein. Unlike Platt, Feinstein was not awesomely precocious. Until age eight, when he beat his electrical engineer father in chess for the first time, he was deemed dyslexic and otherwise slow. But he got over it.

Described by the department head as Caltech's best student in applied mathematics in thirty years, Feinstein talks so fast that Mead coined the "Feinstein" as a unit of speech production and described all other students as speaking in "milli-Feinsteins." Unfortunately, "Feinsteins" slow down to a viscous crawl when translated into writing, and he failed to finish his thesis for several years. When it came, however, it brilliantly illuminated the links between Claude Shannon's information theory and thermodynamics.

Although above all else a mathematician, Feinstein is also deeply philosophical. He can commute readily among such subjects as Jungian psychiatry, the relationship of wave dynamics to the nature of the soul, and the more recherché enigmas of quantum or communications theory. He became the lead teaching assistant and go-between for the course "The Physics of Computation" jointly taught by Hopfield, Mead, and Feynman.

Also influential in Carverland were students who failed readily to make it into the inner circle, but hung around trying to be useful enough to find their way in. One of these was Tim Allen, who had come to Caltech chiefly under the influence of watching Feynman on a tape of a *Nova* program. "I must have played it scores of times," he says. "He didn't have particularly more screen time than any of the others, but there was something about the man I just liked—he was more exciting than any of the others, and hearing him talk about things made me excited about them, too."

Allen's most profound early encounter with technology was a Hewlett-Packard HP-35 scientific calculator, which his physician dad brought home from the office when Tim was nine. "I was old enough to appreciate that arithmetic was difficult and it captivated me to hold something in my hand which was 'smarter than I was.'" Adept at mechanical technology as a boy, he found the calculator "the first thing I had ever encountered whose inner workings were totally impenetrable, invisible, inscrutable. Just a lump of plastic, it didn't whir or click." When he arrived at Caltech nearly a decade later, he chose his courses for their relevance to this machine. He set out to figure out how the HP-35 worked, "all the way to its physical underpinnings."

In his sophomore year he encountered Carver Mead teaching the introductory computer science class, CS10. Mead opened his first lecture with an analogy between the digital computer and a car: "Imagine trying to describe how a car works to a technically savvy alien who'd never seen one before. It would be difficult to believe that an engine that worked by explosions rattling cams up and down could ever produce the outward appearance of smooth quiet motion. Digital computers were the same—frenetic, primitive internal action, well-hidden, causing an illusion of smooth fluid function." Allen concluded, "Carver was articulate, charismatic, and informal, and struck exactly the same chord in me as that videotaped image of Feynman. . . . Caltech had delivered on its promise."

Like his friend Dave Gillespie, Allen was attracted to Carver's Chipmunk lab of HP9836 pre-PCs. Real computer "geeks" disdained the little Chipmunks, preferring to time-share a large centralized near-"mainframe" Digital Equipment "VAX" in the computer center. But Allen and Gillespie quickly discovered that the HP was half as powerful as a VAX and each student had one all to himself, while the VAXes had to be shared with fifty other students. Setting up the Chipmunk lab, Mead showed his grasp of the promise of the *personal* computer back in a period when it seemed a radical idea. This technology has moved so fast that today Allen with his team at Altera Corporation, a major Silicon Valley innovator, has built a microprocessor unit, given away as a promotion, that has the power of 150 VAXes and fits in a corner of one of Altera's chips.

Like Gillespie after him, Allen became a teaching assistant in CS-10. But he still felt that he was on the outside of Carver's more elite lab, looking in. In his senior year, he signed up for Mead's "Analog VLSI and Neural Systems" class, which was largely taught from his forthcoming book by that title. As Allen recalls, "It was new, important, leading-edge glamorous fun, interesting—everything. I experienced the feeling of being in exactly the right place at the right time to catch the perfect wave." But he still had not made his way into Carver's inner circle. To do that, he had to build a custom piece of lab equipment for a silicon retina that was of urgent interest to Carver and a key step on the road to Foveon.

Misha Mahowald gazing into Tobi Delbrück's camera, taking a break from a research conference they attended in 1993. Tobi Delbrück

11

Michelle

Into Mead's band of digital brothers one day in December 1983 strode a woman. Hey, no big deal. She was not the first woman to play an important role in the lab. But the others, such as Telle Whitney before her, and Mary Anne Maher, had been adaptive, supportive, working within the frame, conceiving valuable new digital design tools for advanced transistors. By contrast, this woman, Michelle Mahowald, arrived thinking a transistor was "a kind of radio." She really did. And radios were not her thing.

Michelle was a different kind of woman—an analog woman, some said a "bionic woman," interested in, get this, *gardening*. She was shy at first, but she rather soon began telling Carver what to do . . . and, for nearly ten years . . . she would neither finish her thesis nor leave the laboratory. She would decorate its walls with artsy-dipsy posters, concoct chip designs with an antic hexagonal flare, post lab reports with bright overlapped patches of color, mauves and yellows galore, and release random analog beasts of prey from their safe digital cages. After her passage, the lab would never be the same.

Her landing in the lab was unplanned and unexpected. After the usual prodigies in academics and college boards obligatory at Caltech admissions, she had arrived on the campus three years before from an all-girl Catholic High School in Minneapolis. Full of cautions from her intellectual mother on the perils of the "Californian lifestyle," Michelle was set to study astrophysics and become an astronaut. She wanted to walk in space, transcend her past. She even wanted to change her name, transform her mind. "I wanted to burst out of 'my shell' "—her Michelle Catholic constraints, the concept of original "sin," her structured family, their corseted beliefs, their rules and rosaries. She loved the parents who had adopted her, raised her, and named her Michelle, but she wanted to become "Misha," bionic, lyrical, idyllic, free as a cat in a commune.

She sought to recapture the wonder of a trip to Disneyland at the age of seven, on a ride recalling the Alice of Lewis Carroll or the "incredible shrinking man" of film, or perhaps even Grace Slick's "White Rabbit" pill-borne descent of the 1960s. In the Disney ride, she remembered dwindling down small enough to enter a water molecule, as it bounced around in a Brownian dance. With little Michelle inside, it froze into a dazzling crystal and then melted into a stream, and she thought she was gone for good, flushed down into a Disneyland netherworld, lost in microcellular catacombs, maybe forever. Then she came up face-to-face with a nucleus—a bright red blinking sphere the size of a basketball. Glancing above her she became aware of a gigantic eye, a huge pulsing retina, looking down at her through a microscope, seeming to peer into her mind. Just as Michelle was half giving up hope, half hoping for the ride to last forever, the spectral voice of her guide asked, "Do I dare to go further, into the nucleus?" "Certainly I dare not." And then astonishingly, she began to grow back again . . . could it be . . . recomposing and aggregating the atoms into all the higher levels of structure, cells and blood and bodies, and restoring her to her original size in a conventional family group. There was Papa Al smiling, and embracing her, and Mother Joan, intelligently, judiciously concerned as usual, and sister Sheila, all as before. Her family. But the trip into the molecular microcosm had permanently altered her world. As she recalled, "I thought it all was real. Because you could see the other people on the ride moving in miniature down a tiny plastic pipe, I never thought to doubt."

She concluded: "The world was a much more interesting place than I had been led to believe. There were all these things that were normally invisible to me that were actually there and I found that it was supremely exciting." As the years passed, she imagined that an astronautical trip into space would bring a still more ecstatic high of natural revelation and beauty.

Mahowald's embrace of science was never a mere abstraction. She saw it as a reunion with nature. Unlike her classmates or her associates in the lab, she did not disassemble and rebuild television sets as a child, or construct model planes and rockets, or link with distant lands over ham radios. She painted vivid pictures, with rich colors, consciously suggestive of Picasso. At the age of five, she saw patterns in nature. Pointing happily, she told her father: "Look. The wind blows through the grass and knocks them over like dominoes." She helped plant a maple tree in the backyard and dreamed of having a garden of her own. She hid in her room and gorged on books of fantasy—Tolkien's *Lord of the Rings*, then Hermann Hesse's *Steppenwolf*.

Her teachers and friends from Minnesota remember her as an avid artist and an able gymnast, part of a girls' team that was third in the state. One of her eighth-grade teachers recalls a high moment in kickball. "She just stepped up to the plate and walloped it and it was gone. When I think of Michelle," she said, "I see her standing there, hands together, great big eyes and a shy smile and the kickball zooming out of the park." Her mother remembers her as the most intense and perfectionist of the tap dancers at a local dance studio. Afraid at first to go on stage, nervous and evasive, she emerged once there as a dervish of a dancer. In the audience, they all noticed her, and her mother, Joan, beamed in pride.

Everyone recalls a happy and successful girl, always giving more than expected. But Misha remembers a sense of confinement in her pleasant suburban household and her structured Catholic schools. As a child, "I could not leave through the front door, but I could read books and take that way out." She remembers that at school the teachers tended to devote most of their attention to the slower students, so she again was neglected, and retreated to books and then to college extension courses on a campus near Minneapolis.

Misha never became a typical Caltech science wonk, if such a type can be defined at all on probably the nation's most truly diverse and meritocratic campus. On the plane west to LAX from Minneapolis, headed for college in September 1980 to study physics, she already felt qualms about the usual life of science. By then the little brunette with the theatrical smile and the already fierce intelligence had grown into a big, willowy, owlish girl—what the French call "*jolie laide*," conveying a paradox of coarse features and luminous femininity.

With granny glasses, broad shoulders, a secret forbidden tattoo, and a taste for sixties rock and roll, she comes onto the plane on her way to Caltech with a pile of Conan the Barbarian comics and some colored pencils, given to her by a rakish artist friend Diana. She finds herself sitting next to another youth bound for the campus, flaunting a copy of *Scientific American* and a pile of scientific texts. Sixteen years old, too "nerdy" to believe, "he made me feel old and I wasn't even eighteen." Hormonal, aggressive, splaying peacock plumes of mathematics and physics, he chattered away in the adjoining seat like a runaway proto-professor. Why can't he keep his voltage fields, his calcs, his megahertz, his knees, his vectorials, his Hamiltonians to himself? Why all this mental molestation? Is this going to be the way it is at Caltech? As on several other occasions on her pilgrimage into Southern California's most outré circles of high science, she considered turning back.

In those moments, she would cherish her memory of Minnesota, the quietness of it, the peace. "The seasons were pronounced and you have an acute sense of time passing. In an early-summer day, the sun would shine through the elm leaves bowering the paths along the water, and the light would shimmer and crystallize the scene, and it was as if you could see the trees and grass growing in real time, as if life there has a very short time to live. It has to get it all out of the way in a rush of just three months.

"Then in the winter it is cold but beautiful because the sun is out a lot and ice grows on the branches and the world is made of diamonds. The sense of seasons, of things changing and yet staying the same, isn't there so strongly in California."

AT CALTECH CAME new shocks and changes beyond the ken of Disneyland or the all-girl Catholic High School. Perhaps only her mother really had the picture. Assigned to the Ricketts coed dormitory, she encountered "the sexual dance." Palmy Pasadena resembled something out of Dr. Seuss "with tufted palms trees everywhere and strange gawky animal life and Flowers of Paradise that looked as if they might eat you if you strayed too near." In a college that grants freedom galore for each person to grow up in "his or her own way," meaning virtually no adult supervision, in an institution that did not officially recognize the differences between the sexes, the heat built up.

Misha found herself under a two-year siege by male creatures who resembled her airplane companion, with prognathous math and visible cutaneous oils. Retreating to literature as was her wont, she was taken with the theories of *The Territorial Imperative* of Robert Ardrey and *The Naked Ape* of Desmond Morris, two texts that expound evidence for the theory that most human behavior echoes the ethology of monkeys and baboons. "I was struck by the hypocrisy of the boys, who pretended to be interested in science, in my ideas, but in fact were animals performing rites for my benefit. They were like goats butting heads." For a while, zoology seemed her best guide to life at Caltech.

The jiggling and maneuvering grew intense. They "glommed" onto her and wouldn't let go. "Glomming," so they said, was "a Caltech tradition." The sum of it was that "the guys all wanted to spend more time with me than I wanted to spend with them." All that platonic annealing began to get physical. Only twenty-four hours in a day and 150 male nerds on the floor. These guys wouldn't give up. The neural program was snagged on a high energy plateau.

The sex ratio was seven to one. In war theory, seven to one suffices to overcome almost any armed and entrenched defensive position. For all her brains and heft, physical and intellectual, seven to one was a bit much for Misha. She began to retreat again into "my shell." She was a big girl with an expansive heart, but "there wasn't near enough of me for all of them. I had to learn to slam the door in their faces, to scream at them, or to hide in my room with the lights off, so no one knew I was there."

Often she would flee Ricketts to Dabney, a nearby dorm dominated by the hippy counterculture flourishing at Caltech in a delayed throwback to the sixties. There she met Tim Allen, who when not in Carverland served as a leader in student "government"—"I was like Ralph in *Lord of the Flies*," as he puts it. To him, Misha protested against the behavior of her dorm mates. "I don't think she really trusted me or liked me at first," says Allen today. "I was focused on electrical engineering, making things work, and she wasn't. She was focused on learning about the brain." But the real problem was Caltech's unisex vision. As Allen says, "It was really a case of no-fault, an awkward situation for everyone. It was sad. The guys were not really doing anything wrong. There were just too many of them and they were all doing the same thing and the girls were caught in the middle with no easy way out."

Visiting Dabney, though, she became entranced with Allen's best friend, Tom Tucker. A glowing, charismatic figure, articulate and artistic, one of the most obviously gifted of his class at Caltech, Tucker was deep into everything that Misha's mother feared in "California lifestyles." With Tucker, Misha discovered some of the upside of zoology and the downside of zoological males. Tucker turned out to fascinate many of that year's girls at Caltech. But Misha got more than her share. Together they took her Disneyland hallucinations from physics onto chemistry and pharmacology. From Tucker, she also heard reports of a professor named Carver Mead, whose course Tucker was taking. Like Allen, Tucker was an enthusiast of Mead's adventures in analog VLSI and neuroscience.

Misha still was pursuing physics. But the astrophysics was not going so well. Misha had been a math prodigy back in Minnesota, taking college courses as early as eighth grade. She had read with exhilaration about Caltech's giant observatory at nearby Palomar, with its hyperbolic 200-inch Hale telescope, a kind of Capitol Dome for the university's physicists as they legislate for the universe. When her bus into Pasadena drove past the service entrance to the Caltech Synchrotron Accelerator, where they contrive particle collisions at the speed of light, she thought, "This is it. This is where it really happens. This is where I learn what is really true."

She had always found math easy, and she saw it as a way to prevail in the physical sciences. But at Caltech, everyone was a math prodigy and she discovered that her math gifts were modest by comparison to many of her classmates, more than half of whom were physics majors. She became uneasy with the assumptions they so readily upheld, the idea that all of science was a pyramid, resting on a substrate of physics at the bottom. The physicists implied that everything above was somehow epiphenomenal, that they were merely awaiting some more powerful digital machines to come and subdue the derivative disciplines to the underlying rule of physics.

Plunging into astrophysics, she discovered that the course that she was taking offered little data—reports from Betelgeuse were scant—but bristled with theories and equations. Hard to follow, resting on authority, they made her nervous. Estimates of the total mass in the universe seemed to swell and shrink, back and forth, like an accordion playing an inscrutable modernist tune or like a Disneyland molecule responding to a hidden agenda contrived by men in some remote control center. As an adult, she was losing her faith. She could not tell whether the astrophysical ride was real or not. Inflationary, oscillatory, contractionary, issuing from an ineffable singularity or multiplying into an infinite number of parallel paths, it seemed as if astrophysics were all math, all the time, flying far away into space from the supposedly solid foundations of the physics at the bottom. She had wanted to be an astronaut. Her head was spinning like a nerdy propeller cap, but she was farther than ever from orbit.

In her doubts, she began to notice the patriarchal tradition of Caltech's physics. It resembled nothing so much as the Catholic Church. "All authority seemed to emanate from males." Even the emblem of the space program, a symbol designed to represent life on earth to all other galaxies, showed a man looking forthrightly forward, engaged with the scene, and a woman gazing at him reverently from the side. Was the universe itself a male playground?

In Caltech physics, it seemed to be. She found an introductory biology course more to her taste. Rather than scarce data, bristling masses of equations, and mazes of theory, biology offered reams of data, measurements galore, and a sore need to find patterns in it. She was an artist, adept at patterns. She found herself gravitating toward the living sciences. Science, she concluded, should not be a hierarchy or a pyramid but "an organism, continually growing and changing." Taking a course in neuroscience, she became deeply intrigued by the retina, the sensitive thin outer layer of cells in the eye that receives photons and transduces them into electrons for passage to deeper layers of the brain. In many ways it seemed to offer a path of light into the crypts of the mind. It was a regular structure, well known, with accessible chemistry and self-evident functions. It could be understood. She plunged deep into an effort to master it, and through it to fathom the brain.

In this pursuit, at the beginning of her junior year, she signed up for a course in computational neurophysics. A famous course, begun by Caltech titans Hopfield, Feynman, and Mead, it hoped to achieve a new multidisciplinary synthesis of physics, neurobiology, and engineering, just what Misha was looking for. Hopfield was a mathematical physicist who had turned to biology. Mead was an engineer and physicist with an interest in the brain sciences. Feynman was a legend exploring the limits of computation. But early in Misha's year, he was stricken with cancer and forced to withdraw from the course. That left Hopfield pursuing the neurobiology and neural networks, and Mead expounding on the potential of very large scale integrated circuits for simulating brain functions and performing neural-network-like collective computations.

In the lectures, Misha found Hopfield's ideas inspiring, offering the first plausible path into a model of brain functions—how a simple collection of unintelligent neurons could achieve a form of collective intelligence from the bottom up, with no central control. But she was mostly baffled by Mead's dense explanations of transistor physics. "I couldn't understand him at all," she recalls. Although she demurred at some of the simplifications of Hopfield's neural network model, she decided to do her project on the retina with Hopfield.

She went to meet with the teaching assistant in the course, David Feinstein. Shared and coveted by all the three professors for his extraordinary gifts in mathematical physics, Feinstein had become an emissary among them. Earlier he had reproached them for asking their students to integrate the three disciplines when the three professors themselves seemed to have little idea how the fields could be joined. Then Misha came to him with a paper she had written on the human retina, replete with large drawings that conveyed its operations. She had spent weeks in the Millikan library, hiding away from the Ricketts scene, working out the detail and limning out the supporting art, showing all the biological links and signal pathways, horizontal and vertical. Her model encompassed the entire neural flow of light and energy, from the retinal cones that capture the colors in the eye and the foveal receptors that focus on fine detail such as the letters you are reading, through the triad synapses that begin the communication into the brain and bipolar and amacrine cells in the "plexiform" layers that do vital balancing of energy and dynamics down to the retinal ganglion paths leading to the cortex, which integrates the image into a recognizable whole. From "fan-in" to "fan-out," it was a coherent imaging system.

MISHA WAS SHY about her work, but to Feinstein it seemed an extraordinary vindication of the course. To the physicists Hopfield and Mead, biological science seemed largely guesswork. Nothing in it offered any kind of agenda by which the physiological function could be reproduced. Mahowald was a biologist by training, but she had offered a model of the retina that was at least suggestive of a schematic diagram of a chip . . . a chip that could become a working model of a mammalian eye or a new kind of camera.

*Misha Mahowald shows Carver Mead a feature of the "silicon eye"
that she built in Carver Mead's laboratory. Mead began as Misha's
teacher and ended as her collaborator on the frontiers of brain science.*
Tobi Delbrück

12

Misha

When David Feinstein took Misha to meet with John Hopfield, the prospects seemed favorable for an enduring student-teacher link between the tall, gray-haired professor and the ambitious young biologist. It was Hopfield who had most excited Misha with his model of collective computation by individually dumb neurons in the brain. It was Hopfield whose magnetized "spin glass" concept seemed to offer the possibility of a physical foundation for neuroscience. But Hopfield's neural networks were radically simpler than Mahowald's concept.

Crucially, the Hopfield model was "feed forward." It lacked the feedback loops that were essential to Misha's understanding of a human retina that would have to respond to light over a millionfold dynamic range, from moonlight to midday, that would have to null out vast changes in ambient brightness to focus on the features of a scene.

In talking to Misha, Hopfield too was all feed forward and,

said Feinstein, "in her face." He seemed interested in Misha's retina project only to the extent that it fit with his neural network algorithm. To Misha, if the algorithm did not work for a retina, it could not work for the brain either. She was deeply discouraged and decided to drop the course as irrelevant to her approach to the field.

But Feinstein would not give up. Increasingly intrigued with this woman and her retina, her vulnerable shyness and her powerful intelligence, her capacious smile and her quakes of laughter, Feinstein protested: "This course is supposed to offer a synthesis between biology and engineering. You are the only biologist taking it. If you leave it will be a joke. . . .

"Why don't you show your paper to Carver Mead?" he suggested.

"Oh, no," said Misha, "I can't work with him. I can't understand anything he says. All that electrical engineering. I want to understand the brain."

"He's different in person," Feinstein said. "I'll arrange a dinner."

The next week Mead, Feinstein, and Mahowald met for dinner at the Athenaeum, the old Gothic faculty center at Caltech full of leather chairs, science texts, and men's club smoke. Like hundreds of brilliant students before her, she fell quickly under the spell of Mead's quiet authority and polymathic knowledge. Contrary to what she had expected, amid the smoke, he listened attentively to her views on the retina and grasped immediately their significance. He had been contriving "little toy retinas" himself. He suggested that she do a project with him, working in his lab.

So Misha found herself in the lab surrounded with a mostly different set of males, though Allen, Tucker, and Feinstein were all part of the scene. Mead gave her the kind of guidance and support that she sought. "He was amazing," she said later with a wistful smile. "He had an unworldly intuition of what was likely or possible physically. He could take a phenomenon far beyond his expertise and somehow tell whether it was plausible. In a field like biology, full of conflicting data and speculation, his ability to tell what was physically likely and promising and what was a dead end was crucial. I couldn't have done without it."

Mead's central proposition was that you could not fully understand anything unless you could build it. The biologists offered models of the brain resembling a medieval map of the world, with arrows across the oceans pointing to bodies of land—Broca's region here, area seventeen over there, dragons lurking in a reptilian neural netherworld, and wildly speculative theories connecting one to the other and to the retina. The vessels of interaction might as well have been clipper ships. To an electrical engineer, the biologists had no way of finding out exactly what was going on. They could not implant probes at all the billions of neurons. They could not define the circuitry. They had to use electroencephalograms and nuclear resonance spectroscopy to yield crude patterns of energy flow and then make educated guesses that were impossible to test.

As Feinstein said, "Carver's view of a wiring diagram was on a different planet from the biologists' maps." Mead hoped to build up a primitive brain, piece by piece, beginning with the "transducer physiology," as the elder Delbrück had put it, all the conversions of energy and electrons in retinas and cochleas and the ionic channels that he had studied with the Nobel laureate lion who had strode into his office fifteen years before. When Mead saw Misha's scheme, "it looked like a wiring diagram to me," he said. He could see the possibility of greatly enhancing the sophistication of his electronic models of the retina and actually testing the latest findings of the biologists.

Mead explained: "When we build the circuits and we make them work, make them render images and find edges and adapt to flashes of ambient light, with flows of energy that parallel the brain's, we can understand the retina in a way that the biologists with all their masses of murky measurements never can."

Nonetheless, for several months, they failed in their effort to create retinal devices that could simulate real functions. Under Carver's steady guidance, Misha was learning step-by-step all the soldering, and wiring, and "pin" connections onto an electronic breadboard. Becoming a tyro electrical engineer, she left far behind her original notion of a transistor as mere radio. But they had hit a wall in their understanding of how to translate Misha's general schematic into a wiring diagram that would work.

Meanwhile, over dinners at the Sawmill Restaurant, she was taking Mead through the latest reports from the biologists. As Mead recalls, "She was better than the biologists, because she reinterpreted and embellished their findings as they related to our project." They began by building on Mead's toy retinas. "It is always easier to start with a previous design than to begin with a blank slate," he said. The problem was that the previous retina structures had been designed to perform motion detection—to tell the viewer what was moving in an image rather than merely to present a fixed "picture." At the time, Mead still believed that this function of motion detection was done in analog in the frontal layers of the retina itself. Misha saw it as being done at a deeper level of the brain, in the cortex. The effort to accomplish motion detection on the electronic retinal surface distracted them for two months.

They made key advances, though. Mead showed Misha how to approximate the dynamic range of a real retina—its ability to deal with near darkness and bright sunlight, a difference of a factor of millions—by keeping the light represented by currents rather than translating to voltages. On a chip, voltages are far more convenient, because they can be divided without losing strength, providing "fan-out" crucial for neural models. But currents can vary from picoamps to milliamps, a factor of millions; voltages vary only from milliwatts to five watts, a factor of thousands or less. Mead figured out how to register the intensities by currents and then convert to the logarithm of the voltage. Misha and Mead incorporated this feature in their emerging retinal model that could operate like an eye or a usable camera under conditions of drastically changing light intensities.

At the same time, through Misha's junior year, the pressure in the dorm continued to build up. New troops of baboons arrived. They saw the curvy female semaphore but did not learn to read Misha's feedback. She finally got tired of fending them off. She was an emotional woman and after a tussle at her door, amplified by tears and cries, she had had enough. She rode the

express bus to LAX, got on a plane, and returned to Minneapolis. She was through. She was persuaded to return to Caltech
only when Mead managed to get her scholarship augmented
with money for an off-campus apartment.

Carver did well by the arrangement. Misha became the driving force behind his projects for a retina chip, neuron chip, and
see-hear chip (combining the retina with a cochlea). She aston-
ished the others in the lab with her ability to envisage chip dia-
grams. As one of the leading chip designers, Allen often had to
work with Misha's layouts. "I thought I was good. But she was
better. She was truly gifted with layouts." As Feinstein puts it:
"She had an amazing faculty for spatial visualization: a kind of
intuitive silicon compilation taken to a higher level of the system, with all the feedback loops. She realized what unit cell,
what design primitive, would elegantly generate the entire system. The wiring problem often seemed insurmountable but
Misha was an idiot savant . . . in a good way . . . She called it
'beginner's luck' but she would draw the unit cell and miracu-
lously it would map out into a working system with reflections
and transitions, into a real chip layout." The hexagonal structure
of the retina was her inspiration. As she said: "I began on the
fringe of the lab. Just Carver and I and a retinal model. But by
the end we became the mainstream. Everyone was doing retinas
and cochleas."

Mead's crowded laboratory became chiefly devoted to Max
Delbrück's complex of "transducer physiology"—all the conversions between input from the world and the reflective parts of the
brain. In this pursuit, Misha was in the lead. Sometimes vague,

sometimes vulnerable, Misha, with the capacious Havahart trap of a mind, glommed onto ideas from all the scientific fields that were converging around the lab—neurobiology, electrical engineering, solid-state physics, neural networks, biosensors.

Soon the guys in the lab were eager to share in Misha's projects. Tobi Delbrück collaborated on other retinas and on stereo matching chips that could convey depth of scene. Tim Allen went to work on a device to display the output of Misha's latest retinas in real time on a monitor, rather than downloading the pixels serially and then looking at them later using a plotting program. Mead wanted him to build a system that would scan images from the retina and display them in NTSC television video form, so they could be seen as they happened and adjusted as needed, as in a digital camera. Allen was contemplating various analog video techniques, when disaster struck.

"I was riding my bicycle on Linda Vista Avenue, alongside the Rose Bowl, uphill, drafting behind a friend when he swerved around a parked car. I didn't. My head went through the back window, leaving me badly injured and unconscious. When I woke up in the ambulance, my friend was with me. I remember asking him two questions: 'Did I get into Stanford?' (Yes.) 'Am I going to make it?' . . . Nervous looks all around."

It turned out most of the damage was facial and required reconstructive surgery. The incident left him some scars and cost him three weeks at the lab. By the time he got back, the leisurely project for Misha and Carver had become an emergency. He lamented his plight with another student, who responded off-the-cuff: "Just use a ROM (digital read only memory)." The ROM could store a digital numerical scheme of the TV conversion algorithm. It didn't all have to be done in analog, without numbers, with all the changes performed in continuous electrical patterns hard to store and control.

As Allen put it: "Instantly, I could see the entire solution. All the complexity of the video scanning process, and even the waveform itself, could be encoded in a ROM. A trivial digital circuit could read the ROM contents out and drive the retina chip and a few key inputs on the mixer for the image." He built the circuit in a day and spent the next week creating a program to generate the ROM contents in NTSC video format.

As a result, Allen became something of a hero in the lab. Video sources made on a breadboard are notoriously sloppy: jumpy synch, blurry pixels, lots of noise. But the ROM digital approach made everything predictable with rock-solid timing, crisp pixel boundaries, and a clear picture. "Carver and Misha were both thrilled with the results. I had crossed the boundary between 'peripheral character' and one of the Chosen in the lab." As Carver put it later, giving him the ultimate Caltech compliment: "Tim, you really grokked it." No one thought it especially significant that he had grokked it by going digital—by separating the computation from the changing real values of the image and converting them all into numbers synchronized to a clock pulse.

DURING THIS PERIOD in her senior year, Misha's relationship with Feinstein grew ever more intense. Lovers and intellectual explorers, they would talk deep into the night, about philosophy, engineering, biology, the nature of the brain, the power of religion and spirituality. Driving in Feinstein's big Corvette, with its sumptuous black leather seats, they would return to park outside Misha's apartment around midnight and sometimes not leave the car until five, engrossed in each other, yes, but even more entranced with the incandescence of their intellectual pursuits. Leaving "Michelle" behind at last, Misha had found a new academic father in Carver, supporting her work, and an intellectual and romantic companion in Feinstein, nurturing and stretching her mind. With two of the best minds at Caltech at her service, she was feeling at home in the world for perhaps the first time.

There was, however, a persistent canker of dissatisfaction. To the world, the Caltech program of putting brain functions in silicon was advancing with amazing speed. Mead's laboratory had become globally famous in the field. But to Misha, their progress in understanding the brain seemed agonizingly slow and she continued to pursue—against Feinstein's warnings—what she saw as the parallel path of drugs.

Cocaine, she found, gave her an inspiring feeling of completeness, as if all her work were done, all her challenges overcome. Heroin she tried once and gave up. LSD was her favorite, and it did indeed reproduce in an eerie way the feeling of wonder and discovery that she remembered from Disneyland. But perhaps her most powerful insights came from the ingestion of THC (tetra-hydro-cannabinol)—the essence of marijuana—in brownies.

Feinstein remembers sitting in the car with her late at night, while she exclaimed that she could count the photons reaching her eye. She had a vivid and overwhelming sense of the paucity of the information from which her brain was creating a rich tapestry of nocturnal sights. From just a few scant photons, massless messengers, her mind could build a scene full of mass, detail, and beauty. The experience strengthened her conviction that vision is an achievement of an entire mind—that it reached far beyond the retinal models she was building.

The retina could not do it alone. She would have to explore the farthest shores of consciousness itself. . . .

COMPLETED OVER SEVEN years under Carver's wing, Mahowald's doctoral thesis in 1992 won the Clauser award for the best Caltech thesis of the year. The first woman ever to win that prize at Caltech, she even relieved some of her mother's fears about California by giving her "the most exciting day of my life" when the award was announced, the last and most prestigious prize of the year. They dined that night at the Athenaeum with Carver Mead and Francis Clauser, the physicist who had donated the award. Misha reassured her mother that she had joined the John Henry Newman Society, a gathering of Caltech Catholic women who also pursued yoga and spiritualism.

As Misha went on her triumphant way, writing articles, chapters, books, she was called by WGBH of Boston and in 1993 submitted to some twelve hours of interviews for a documentary on her life. Entitled "Silicon Visions," it was shown in May 1995 for a full hour on PBS, as part of the science series *Discovering Women*, and was narrated by Michelle Pfeiffer.

Coming from biology into the dense mathematical briar patches of Caltech physics and engineering, she was sympathetic with other newcomers in the field. Writing *Microcosm*, I would consult Misha when I needed a clear explanation of some issue of the science. I found her a dazzling mix of contradictions. Earnest, wistful, ambitious, and modest, all at once—a biologist, a physicist, an engineer, an experimenter with drugs—she pushed her brain in so many directions that some of the time she did not seem all there. But through it all, she was following the complex paths of Mead's science farther perhaps than any of his other students did.

I remember walking behind her for hours, watching the big brown braid bounce on her back, as we climbed the sepia hills above Pasadena. Here she often retreated to ponder the convergence between her biological studies and her physics, and here she went from time to time with women friends from the Newman club. It comforted her, she told me, "to reflect that my biological creatures all perform amazing mathematical feats all the time." She waved away a curious fly. "Yes, this fly," she said, "can see and react faster than the largest supercomputer while using a billionth of the power. I spent six years at Caltech learning the Schrödinger equation, but the merest electron can solve the Schrödinger equation all day long. That is what it does—its every movement embodies that calculation. It does not even know it's hard." Through many permutations, Misha's early work on the retina chip would lead in the end to Foveon. But it would be hard.

Misha was a scientist first. While many of her colleagues in

Carverland went north to companies in Palo Alto and Santa Clara, Misha would not become a Silicon Valley girl. She kept her eye on the fly. When she was offered a leadership post in an eminent neurobiological laboratory at Oxford University in England, she accepted it eagerly. Misha had changed Carverland. Now she was off to change the world of biology.

Federico Faggin at a desk at Synaptics with a lot of electronic equipment that he would eventually make obsolete. Did the rose come from Carver Mead? Alvia? Courtesy of Federico Faggin

13

Synaptics

It was not only Misha who was impressed by the thinking prowess and neurophysical charms of flies. Mead's laboratory was one of the few places on the face of the earth where all the humans bowed humbly to the brain of the lordly Diptera. Dipterolatry ruled, and it was driving some of them to drink and other distractions.

In the lab, Tim Allen, for example, imagined that he could deploy thousands of times more processors than a fly, millions of times more connectivity and hugely more power. And he was not speaking of any artificial neural network. He was referring to his own mental faculties. Yet he remains baffled by the eye, brain, and nervous system of a fly. It swats aside all the notions of neuromorphic insight that from time to time were claimed in this elite laboratory, which was widely known to be leading the world in the electronic emulation of neural functions.

With its tiny brain and infinitesimal metabolism, the fly easily eludes Allen's hand, and only by mustering all his concentration and effort can he sometimes hit it with a swatter. It would be like someone hitting him with the Transamerica Building. Yet much of the time little Diptera gets away. By any obvious measure, the fly's brain is less complex than one of Allen's advanced Application Specific Integrated Circuits (ASICs). Yet with autonomous power, the fly performs maneuvers that would be the envy of any aerobatic team with the most advanced airplanes commanding the computing power of scores of thousands of ASICs. The fly can do flawless flip landings on the edge of a glass or on a glass ceiling while scarcely slowing down. It can find food out of thin air from elusive chemical cues. All the Caltech computer firepower in Carver's lab—Misha's retina and Lyon's see-hear chip, David Gillespie's computer-aided engineering, David Feinstein's mathematical virtuosity, John Platt's neural networks, Tobi Delbrück's prowess and creativity with analog electronic circuitry—could not even scratch the surface of the evident superiority, and continuing inscrutability, of the eye, brain, and nervous system of the fly.

As Allen finished up his career at Caltech in 1987, he still hoped to learn how the fly's brain worked. No obvious quantitative measure explained it. The fly's neurons were more densely interconnected than any silicon chip. But they operate millions of times more slowly. And a million neurons, however heavily interlinked, could not in themselves perform the fly's repertory using any principles of artificial intelligence or neural network algorithm known to computer science.

The real target of the researchers in Carver's lab was the human brain. Although a lummox by comparison, the human brain offered far more formidable challenges. Its capabilities, so Allen believed, must similarly stem from as-yet unknown structural principles, independent of its substrate (or substance), since it operates with continuity over a period of decades while its cells constantly alter in an environment with ever-changing temperatures and other conditions. For example, how does the brain retain memories for fifty years or more, while the substance of the cells is replaced and the body endures thousands of environmental shocks and transformations? Analog? Digital? Quantum? Or an abstruse synthesis of all three? Who knew? Mead, Hopfield, or Feynman? Don't ask them. Allen thought that there had to be some architectural concept, some principle of neural organization, that was eluding the group. If only they could find it, what laurels they could win. . . .

Hoping to continue the quest, he applied to graduate school at Caltech. Like most Caltech graduates, he was accepted only if he spent a year somewhere else, either working or studying. It seemed that he would have to leave the brain science challenge with Misha who then, in 1987, was still in Pasadena. Allen now seriously needed a job, and Silicon Valley was just slowly emerging from its mid-1980s crash. Living in his VW van, he posted forty rejection letters on the bulletin board in the lab. It was a cry for help. Finally, he turned in desperation to Carver Mead. Although Mead followed a rule of never recruiting directly from his lab, he would respond to students who made specific inquiries. Mead told Allen about Synaptics and dazzled Allen with the exploits of the legendary Faggin, creator of the first microprocessors at Intel, and, at Zilog, the Z-80.

"The Z-80, wow," said Allen. "I learned to program on a Trash 80—that Radio Shack box that used the Z-80. It's my favorite microprocessor." That was a start. It was not as amazing as a fly, but at least he could understand how it worked. He was excited by the idea that the designer of the Z-80 now believed that comparable advances could be made in neural networks.

SYNAPTICS WAS A fancy new neural name for a small pile of venture capital lamely launched the year before as Meno Corporation by aspiring venturer Lauren Yazolino. For help in finding a fashionable product, Yazolino called Faggin, then a high-powered consultant, who suggested his old dream of a microprocessor based on neural networks. Since the company had no CEO, Faggin was asked to take over and he did. In the new world of neural processing, the monicker Meno did not convey the cachet or the concept. Faggin suggested Synaptics, and it stuck. To find a neural network expert, he called his old colleague Mead in October 1986, and together they began to assemble a team. In Synaptics literature, Faggin and Mead are described as the founders, Faggin as the initial CEO and Mead as chairman.

Arriving at Synaptics in suite 106 in an office complex on Zanker Road in Santa Clara, Allen became the first employee of the reorganized company. Glenn Gribble, a software expert in the Caltech lab as an undergraduate, followed him a month later. Joining Faggin in the small laboratory, Allen planned to continue the neuromorphic pursuit. As time passed, many of his previous colleagues from Caltech joined him: Tom Tucker, David Gillespie, Adam Greenblatt, Janeen Anderson, John Platt, Ting Kao, Lloyd Watts. Platt had served as an intern at the Schlumberger Artificial Intelligence Lab with Dick Lyon, who also dropped in once or twice, though he first became a competitor, designing handwriting recognition devices at Apple. Tobi Delbrück was a regular visitor.

Meeting from time to time at dinners in the Valley with Mead and Faggin, Misha came by in the summer of 1987 and pronounced them a "dynamite team." Allen took her in his VW bus to a Grateful Dead concert at Laguna Seca in Monterey. She was happy and at home, as at ease in the hippy scene and its funny smoke as she was intense under the rigors of Caltech graduate school and her emerging thesis on the retina. Carver himself spent one day a week in the office. Synaptics seemed to be becoming Carverland North.

Allen never did get around to reentering Caltech. "The first few years at Synaptics, I was doing the same work as Misha and Tobi, except I was well paid, better equipped, and got more individual attention from Carver."

Yet Faggin was growing increasingly uneasy. By March 1987, Mead had yet to point to a marketable idea from his laboratory. Carver was still coming in only one day a week. The imagers were toys. The neural networks could not perform real computing. Although *Business Week* would identify the Synaptics technology as one of the five leading innovations of 1987—that was the kind of hype Carver could generate—no serious applications had emerged. Faggin had to return to the venture capitalists with the news that he was reorganizing the company in "research mode." He explained: "It is going to take a long time, this neural stuff. Not a lot of money, but a lot of time."

IN THE ANNEALING model, every technology company needs two kinds of leadership, coming from two kinds of men. Let's call them, for short, the Meads and the Faggins.

One is mercurial, imaginative, philoprogenitive, conceiving of something new and bringing it to life, often initially malformed and precarious, but loving it as a mother does. He sees infinite potential in the balky bundle, in a fuzzy-faced sophomore with quirky design tools, in the noisy breadboard, in the oversized and slow imager chip, in the large young bio major with granny glasses, in the snarl of wires and switches. Optimistic, risk taking, often less than punctilious, sometimes sentimental, he pursues the top line—running from wistful hope to fitful revenues—and often wins the credit of the crowds if the venture succeeds. If it doesn't, don't bother him; he is off on something else.

This man could not consummate his ideas without collaborators, also creative and resourceful, but at a lower level of abstraction. Where the Mead is visionary, the Faggin is skeptical. Where the Mead is seeing "zero-billion-dollar" markets, the Faggin is looking for initial nine-dollar sales. Where the Mead is all peripheral vision, seeing the interconnections among everything in his universe, the Faggin dons blinders and bends toward the bottom line, the goal line, profits now . . . And that baby in the bathwater, that recognizer chip with the blurry images, it was a hopeless kludge.

Though needing each other, the two types may sometimes pretend to hold all the virtues in their singular selves. Even when the claims are true—both Mead and Faggin, after all, are Renaissance men of our era—they may not be able to combine the roles in practice during the course of eighteen-hour days. When these two types conflict, their company suffers. But when the two forms of leadership align themselves synergistically, they can unleash an unstoppable force.

Carver Mead with his protégé Tim Allen at Allen's wedding in Novem-
ber 1990. Allen was Mead's student at Caltech and the savior of the
touch-pad project at Synaptics. Courtesy of Tim Allen

14

The Analog Perplex

Tim Allen saw the first two years of Synaptics in 1987 and 1988 as an exploratory phase. Allen and Glen Gribble had set up the lab, developed design tools for neural networks, and experimented with several neuromorphic analog circuits. Tom Tucker joined for a while and made contributions, but seemed incapable of focusing on this long-term project. He left and did not return. People came and went. Faggin had a point. Perhaps Synaptics resembled too much a Carverland lab. It turned out, as Allen recalls, that "all we had done was run down our money. Understanding the brain was just a subject too deep for ten guys and ten Sun workstations to figure out. By 1989, we knew it was time for a commercial application of some sort."

At that point, the company began a sharp expansion. Allen's good friend Dave Gillespie saw fit to leave Carverland south and follow the others up Route 5 to Synaptics. Gillespie brought tremendous sophistication in computer science and chip design to the project. He replaced Glenn Gribble, who had stormed out of the company after an obscure but intense row with Faggin. In April, John Platt finished his Ph.D. thesis for Carver (on graphics applications of neural networks), crammed his belongings into an Oldsmobile, and drove to Silicon Valley. He enlisted as employee number six, on the way to becoming chief scientist. He and Faggin soon began collaborating on original research on "Blind Source Separation," an abstruse field, which used complex time delay algorithms to improve identification of the *sources* of sensor signals such as sounds mixed up in passage— for example, the output of an array of microphones. Presented at NIPS4, a neuroscience conference, these innovations led to the creation of a mathematically esoteric research field still flourishing today.

Although the company had yet to achieve a saleable product beyond its own unique research, Synaptics was one of the most closely watched and celebrated start-ups in the Valley. Large revenues and profits seemed just a matter of time.

THEN IN 1991, everything changed for the Synaptics band of brothers. Verifone called, proposing a major application for the technology. No more flies, no more abstruse neuroscience, no more visits from Misha then finishing up at Caltech, no more Carverland North.

With a billion dollars of revenue, Verifone was the leading company in point-of-sale credit-card readers. Now it was aiming to introduce a device to read the MICR (magnetic image character recognition) codes on the bottoms of checks. Just as you currently swipe your credit card through a reader, so in the future you could swipe a check. Joining the two key areas of expertise of the company—image processing and neural networks—the new Verifone device would combine a fast image scanner with two neural devices, one to find the MICR codes on the check and the other to read the numbers. The imager would be based on the retina work at Caltech, including Misha's ingenious edge recognizer circuit. It enabled devices to detect light, identify edges, and look for patterns. The neural nets would use "a fiendishly ingenious algorithm" from John Platt, based on a recent invention called a Support Vector Machine. He also designed a training algorithm for the device that could process the equivalent of 128 thousand examples in 7.5 minutes on a Sun Sparc 2 server. Storing the synaptic weights on the chip would be floating-gate technology pioneered by Faggin.

Allen was in charge of developing the analog floating-gate technology. But when Faggin broached the idea to the company's foundry—UMC in Taiwan, which would have to make the chips—the engineers just said, "No." Floating gates for flash memory cells that each could hold a single bit, identifiable only as a one or zero, with nothing in between, had been devilishly difficult to perfect. UMC had to guarantee the memory's endurance over fifteen years, and it had taken the company almost ten years to make it reliable. Now that they had the reliability statistics and the working design at last, the foundry was *not* going to mess with it. Faggin's idea of a floating gate that could hold not a *number* (based on binary ones and zeroes) but a *continuous* fractional analog weight over time without leakage or degradation—this was beyond the capabilities of the UMC process.

At Caltech, they had always been able to program the synaptic connectors among the neural net's neurodes with memories in a computer plugged into the wall (that was real nonvolatility) or with electronic potentiometers (like continuous light dimmers). But Verifone wanted a cheap single-chip system that could be bolted to the side of the cash register and would keep its weights if you turned it off. Allen explored the possibilities of solving the problem with some other device, but he had hit a mental barrier. There were a lot of ideas—ferroelectric this and that, amorphous silicon circuits—but nothing was near ready except a return to old-fashioned magnetic cores and no one made those anymore. Faggin's basic concept for a programmable single-chip neural net processor seemed to be far out of reach.

Allen remembers driving up Route 17 from his home in Santa Cruz in a rental car with Mead discussing the problem. "Carver always had a rental car because he flew up from Caltech every week and stayed at a motel in Sunnyvale." Contemplating various solutions, Mead said: "The simplest way to do it, of course"—Allen liked that "of course"—"would be to program the weights as different transistor sizes. We know we can do that." That was the solution. It would not be a reprogrammable chip, but the MICR marks in the bar codes on the checks consisted of numbers that would not change—just have to read from zero to nine, plus four code blips. It would be an application-specific device that could find the codes and recognize them.

During this period, the company contracted to do a series of such projects. It signed up with a bank to do a cash counter that could both gauge the number of bills in a pile and also read the amount of each one, and it committed to contrive address label readers for the Post Office and for United Parcel Service. Faggin made a deal with a scanner company called Caere to do a detector for an Optical Character Recognition wand. These projects had baffled many companies in the past, but neural networks and neuromorphic imagers made them accessible at last.

Meanwhile, some of the limitations of the chip they had made for Verifone were coming to the fore. Perhaps all MICR codes were not the same after all. On a cue from Verifone, Allen visited the bad-check repository of the 7-Eleven convenience store chain. It was a large one-story warehouse in Dallas. Millions of bad checks. Allen got permission to swipe bounced checks through the machine to his heart's content. One thing became clear right away. They had been working from a highly idealized rendition of the MICR codes. They were all supposed to be the same, but in the real world there was a host of subtle variations and a lot of the time the machine did not work. They had to go back to the drawing board and change the design to accept more variety, which meant changing the sizes of the transistors and also possibly increasing the number of mistakes. Where were the floating gates when they needed them? Well, standard floating gates were good enough to store a rough value, and that would be good enough for a neural network. The forte of neural networks, after all, was dealing with imprecise inputs. That was why you used them, what they were for.

Employing the standard process used for digital memory cells in erasable programmable read only memories (EPROMs), a floating gate could store an analog charge with the equivalent of perhaps six bits of resolution (which in a binary system means a number of two to the sixth, or sixty-four gradations of accuracy). That was exciting; that was good enough for the synaptic weights of a neural network that could recognize codes. What was anyone waiting for? "Well," Allen mused one day, in the lingo of his trade, "if I just took 6 bits of digital memory, I could store the charge with the same accuracy. Of course, I'd need Analog to Digital converters and D to As. That is a hassle. Perhaps you would not go digital for 6 bits. But with just a measly 12 bits of standard EPROM cells I could store two to the twelfth or 4,096 bits of resolution. That's three orders of magnitude more and still just the one A to D. Maybe there is something in this digital stuff after all." Analog seemed to work only in fixed applications, when the algorithm or inputs do not change. If you need memory or programming, you still needed to turn to digital.

Nonetheless, as Mead, Platt, Allen, and Gillespie all agree, with altered transistor sizes the check-reading device began working robustly. As Platt recalls: "We really sweated blood to get the . . . chip working in time for Verifone's shipping schedule. We only had a few people . . . so everyone helped out and did work that was far outside their normal job description. To meet deadlines for our silicon foundry, all of the engineers in the company pulled a simultaneous all-nighter, going through pot after pot of strong coffee, to make sure that the first version of the chip went out on time and correct." Platt, the neural network guru and computer science Ph.D., became "chip verification guy."

"I was frantically entering VLSI schematics into our CAD System while Tim Allen was laying the chip out. That's life at a start-up," Platt remembers.

Called the I-1000, the chip fulfilled all the specifications of Verifone, reading the hardest MICR codes with an accuracy of 99.995 percent. Integrating a variety of leading-edge analog and neural network technologies on a single chip, it seemed to be a dazzling triumph of the Synaptics vision. But what's this? Verifone's specs were changing. That was not part of the plan. Verifone wanted a cheaper chip. Verifone's customers wanted a motor to pull the checks through the machine, which was precisely what the optical reading chip was engineered to avoid (with a motor you don't need a smart optical imager; a motor can precisely pull the check past an ordinary magnetic reader). The Verifone executives who had approved the project left. For whatever reason, the deal fell through.

Faggin says today that it was a good thing in retrospect, because the analog settings on the chip would have deteriorated in use and it would have been "a bitch to keep in the field." No one else on the project has any idea what he is talking about. Faggin's growing disenchantment with analog devices has apparently jaded his memory of his successes in launching them. In any case, the chip used delta-based or differential technology that maintained accuracy under any conditions that would not also destroy a digital device. But even by Faggin, its ultimate author, the virtues of the I-1000 are less remembered today than the collapse of the market for it. Retrospect is like that.

After the Verifone fiasco, similar frustrations afflicted the other projects. Unable to create a general-purpose neural network processor with programmable synaptic weights, the Synaptic devices became special-purpose custom chips, each taking some two years to develop and each only good for one application. Even with changeable synaptic weights, the difficulty remained. For recognizing numbers, a ten-item matrix was optimal, but for letters you needed twenty-six, regardless of how variable the synaptic weights were. Similar problems afflicted almost every neural architecture and application. It turned out that neural nets were parallel processors, and as Carver had been teaching for fifteen years, "parallel processing is inherently application specific."

But all these obstacles to the analog ambitions of Mead and Faggin were trivial compared to the real showstopper on Zanker Avenue. During those two years while Allen, Gillespie, Platt, and the others perfected their special-purpose analog devices, the world's ten thousand digital chip designers had more than doubled the capability of digital technology. They generated some two hundred thousand new digital designs. Faggin pointed out, "Just think what we were competing against. Between 1986 and now, Intel has increased the clock rate of digital from 50 megahertz to 3 gigahertz." By the time Synaptics would present its amazingly ingenious and low-power little analog chip, Verifone, Caere, the Post Office, or the bank—whoever the customer happened to be—had come up with a high-power digital solution that was good enough and that could be simply plugged in to an IBM PC.

It was not only Synaptics that fell before this cycle. Faggin tells the story of CTI, a company that makes telephone terminal equipment. During the same period in the early 1990s, it managed to bring to market an analog serial memory that could displace the tape recorder in a phone answering machine. It was cheap, robust, nonvolatile, and good enough to record fifteen seconds or more of talk in its first rendition. Then the DRAM memory producers began to search for markets for their defective chips. For most digital computing applications a defective memory cell, or row, was a killer. But for a voice recording, no one could tell the difference. However ingenious CTI's analog system might be, it could not compete with an analog-to-digital converter and billions of nearly free reject chips from DRAM fabs. If you needed nonvolatility, add a battery. As Faggin observed sardonically: "The world has many cylinders."

Gillespie concludes, "This experience led to a lot of soul-searching around here. For linking to the real world, analog is indispensable. But trying to build analog circuits to do a computation that could be done digitally is to fight City Hall. You are going to lose. If you need to compute, go to Fry's and buy a computer."

With all Silicon Valley trooping to Fry's, the company had reached an impasse. By 1992, all its contracted projects were on the road to failure. The Post Office, Caere, United Parcel Service, the cash counter all were kaput. Faggin and Mead, though, each had one further project under way. Mead was doing CMOS imagers, with the goal of developing his retina technology into a new analog camera that would collect all the color information accurately and usurp film. Mead said Tobi Delbrück's imager work was "extremely promising."

Having watched Carver's analog systems come to nothing over the previous six years, however, Faggin was incredulous. Regardless of any Delbrück miracles, competing with the $20 billion camera industry seemed to be more than merely ambitious. Let's just say "impossible." Or maybe crazy. But Faggin had served for ten years on the board of Logitech Corporation, the computer interface device company. There, two years before, he had come up with a better idea.

Dave Gillespie at his office, with one of his Synaptics touch pads visible behind his right shoulder. From the iPod to the "teleputer," Gillespie sees ever-rising markets for "haptic" devices. Dave Gillespie

15

Seizing the Sword

As Peter Drucker has written, in any industry the largest profits tend to go to the company which supplies the missing element that completes a system.

Located in Freemont, California, across the bay from Silicon Valley, Logitech Corporation was doing well as a maker of computer mice and trackballs (essentially upside-down mice) that completed desktop computer systems. On the Logitech board, however, Federico Faggin had come to understand that these technologies would not suffice for notebook computers. Pretty soon notebook computers would be most of the business, and they still had no adequate input device.

Trackballs took too much space and depth, gummed up with moisture, and, if you tried to clean one in an airplane, would be likely to fall out and roll under the seats to the other end of the cabin. If a stewardess stepped on one, the coffee, tea, or milk might go flying—not a useful cursor effect. IBM had concocted a little track-stick that avoided the moisture problem, but it stuck up through the keyboard and gave you the IBM finger—if you thought that way—whenever you made a mistake, which many people did as the cursor gyrated wildly across the screen.

With Logitech engineers, Faggin came up with the idea of a computer touch pad and had persuaded the Logitech board to adopt it. After an exhaustive worldwide search, he found the perfect company to build the chip to run the device. It was a little firm across the bay called Synaptics. Indeed, Synaptics probably had the best skills for designing a system that could recognize a finger position robustly and accurately. Such a device would have to be analog, and it would have to have significant powers of pattern recognition such as were uniquely afforded by neural networks.

To pursue this opportunity, Faggin proposed a partnership between Logitech and Synaptics. Logitech already had the drivers and firmware to connect the device to the PC and the sales force to market it to the PC industry. Although Faggin's thrill of invention was dampened when he investigated the patent record and found 170 examples of "prior art," no one had yet managed to put the touch-pad idea into practice. After all, there had been plenty of "prior art" ideas for the microprocessor also.

Early in 1992, Faggin signed a contract with his friends at Logitech, Per Luigi Zapacosta and Giacomo Marini—"the Italian connection"—and their Swiss colleague, Daniel "Bobo" Borel. The group settled on price parameters for a two-chip solution, including a Motorola microcontroller, with plans to move to a single device when volumes rose. Steve Bisset, a Silicon Valley veteran who had begun at Intel and defected in 1976 to form chip-tester pioneer Megatest, had joined Synaptics as a marketing VP in 1989. Faggin put him in charge of coordination with the Logitech engineers.

Bisset's greatest contribution was the idea of dispensing with the need to attach the touch pad to the computer as another layer of gadgetry. He suggested that they move the touch-pad capacitors into the back of the computer's printed circuit board itself. Circuit-board layers had become so thin that they could accommodate the entire sensor array, enabling an entirely integrated touch pad. Taking virtually none of the precious space inside the computer, one side of the pad would bear the chips and connectors, surface mounted on a printed circuit card inches square. The other side of the card would provide the surface space where you place your finger.

Faggin led the planning and assigned the design job to Bisset's new hire Bob Miller, a burly six-foot-four Caltech graduate from Intel who was uncontaminated by the earlier failures. Consulting with Mead, Miller learned the magic of analog. He designed a system with analog potentiometers, floating gates, and other novel circuitry. The chip fit Synaptics technology well. As Faggin says, "It was close to the teaching of Carver, with analog sensors and recognizers and compensation using floating-gate devices." Faggin, Bisset, and Miller got patents on the device.

Soon plunged into a bitter divorce, however, Bisset came to Faggin and asked to leave the project. He needed time to reflect and nurse his wounds. He asked for a part-time job. Faggin could not accommodate him at Synaptics—one key part-timer, Carver, seemed enough—but when Bisset suggested that he move to Logitech and manage the project part-time from the other side, Faggin saw a "win-win" for both companies. He intervened at Logitech to make the arrangement. Bisset moved to Logitech and was put in charge of the touch pad. By early 1992 the prototypes came back from the foundry and worked well enough to signal a go for the project. Faggin went to Logitech to finalize the deal.

It was then that his friends at Logitech began to get shifty. They told Bob Miller they wanted a drastically lower price that would take nearly all the profit out of the product. As Gillespie puts it, "It was the classic situation for a joint venture to fail. We had this device which had a lot of added value and we wanted to make a profit, while Logitech had all the key interfaces and market connections and wanted the chip at cost."

Faggin thought he could straighten out his longtime colleagues. After all, it had been Faggin who had conceived the touch-pad opportunity for Logitech in the first place. But his Italian connection had frayed, as Per Luigi and Giacomo had resigned from management and Daniel "Bobo" Borel had taken over. On the Logitech board, Faggin had long supported Bobo and gotten along well with him. As a last resort, Faggin decided to pull out all the stops and resolve the issue man-to-man. Meeting Borel for breakfast at the Stanford Court Hotel in Menlo Park, Faggin thought they were near agreement. Faggin would just patiently explain the cost situation, and as soon as Bobo understood the deal would be done.

Every time Faggin tried to pin down the terms, however, Bobo would shift ground. Like Oliver Twist, he always wanted "more."

Borel believed that Synaptics had no recourse. "We were cornered," said Faggin. But as creator of the first microprocessor and an industry paladin, he was not going to run a profitless contract design house for Logitech Corporation. He knew he was crazy. But his pride got the best of him. He stood up at the table and announced that the two companies would have to go their separate ways. Yes, he was resigning from the Logitech board. He would figure out some course for Synaptics. Bye, bye, Bobo.

Back at Zanker Road, Faggin summoned all his team for a company meeting. After much wrangling and many questions, he called for a crash effort to create an entire touch pad, complete with drivers, firmware, ergonomics, and even economics, that could be designed, built, and sold by Synaptics. If they could not win by joining Logitech, they would win by beating them. This meant a complete life change for the company. Forget understanding the brain, forget exotic imagers, forget the comforts of Carverland. Faggin was leading the company into the fierce, unforgiving crucible of competition in the global personal computer business. If you didn't like it, well, you could leave. He had the board on his side. And one by one, many of the previous stalwarts did indeed leave.

Faggin's decision might not have seemed as foolhardy as Mead's idea of competing with Kodak, Nikon, Canon, and Sony, but it was close. Logitech had Steve Bisset and his intimate knowledge of the Synaptics design. From long experience in the mouse business, Logitech had the crucial and time-consuming firmware and software drivers to connect to any personal computer. And Logitech had close ties to every major manufacturer of personal computers, including the inscrutable webs of Taiwanese fabs and contract manufacturers and obscure but crucial niche PC players elsewhere in Asia.

Alps in Japan was already well on the way to producing a touch pad for PCs. Moreover, one of those 170 patent holders that Faggin had found turned out to be a company called Cirque in Salt Lake City, and they had already tied up a contract for Apple's new Powerbook. Synaptics seemed to have almost no chance. But in the face of the definitive failure of its other designs and the quixotic prospects of the imager project, Faggin could present "almost no chance" as a tempting new horizon of opportunity. Battered by long failure, the board did not balk. Nearly everyone was willing to "bet the company" on something, and if Faggin thought touch pads were the ticket, they would buy another ride. At the least, touch pads meant competing with Logitech and various companies they had scarcely heard of rather than with Nikon or Kodak.

Allen and Gillespie also supported Faggin's decision. But until this meeting the touch-pad project had been a fringe operation at Synaptics. "An 'ugly duckling,' " as Gillespie said, "without elegant neural nets or imagers." Allen and Gillespie were focused on speech recognizers, pattern matchers, retinas, neural functions. Enthralled by all this high science, everyone was willing to let Faggin, Bisset, and Bob Miller, all old Intel hands, have their way with this low-rent project. But when Allen finally scrutinized "all the gory details" of Miller's design, his stomach began to churn ominously. As he thought about it more deeply, he was ready to scream, "Not again!" He concluded that Miller's design would bring the company down.

Through the Verifone episode, the Post Office fiasco, UPS, Caere scanners—through all the gay launches and gory denouements—Allen had annealed a set of rules for marking the boundaries between analog and digital. The direct interfaces with the world all had to be analog. So the finger would have to be sensed and located through analog circuitry—through a capacitor matrix. A capacitor is two conductors separated by an insulator. A finger is essentially "a bag of water," a conductor, and the sensor array would be conductive. The finger would move, and the capacitors would discharge and issue a rough pattern of data that could ultimately define the point on an x/y capacitive matrix. All these sensory functions would be analog.

Allen's rule was that analog was fine for signals with time constants on a scale of milliseconds. The charge would not degrade or leak away before you had to use it. Filtering and comparison circuits could often be done in analog, since they operate passively and fast. But if the time spreads toward a second, you have to go digital. A touch pad would have to remember the finger's placement for as long as a minute or more—people *rest* their fingers on the pad. It could not forget where the finger was. It could not forget the residual pattern when the finger was absent. Bob Miller intended to store these values on analog floating gates designed into electronic potentiometers. Allen saw floating gates as nothing but trouble. They would drift and distort the output, assuring failure.

Tim Allen felt his job was on the line. But forming in his mind was the entire circuit diagram of a device that could succeed, a device that might even prevail in the market. He called Dave Gillespie and invited him to come up the next day to his place near Santa Cruz above Route 17 to help him define the details. Allen himself had conceived and helped design the house. A mostly glass structure on a ridge 3,000 feet high at the top of Soda Springs Road, it was "all analog," as Allen put it. "You could not change it." Through the windows on a good day, you could see from Monterey to San Francisco, from Bay Bridge to Pebble Beach. But this was not a good day. There was a wild storm outside, rain beating in torrents against the glass. Even an ordinary storm in the valley would bring 80-mile-per-hour winds at the top of the ridge. Allen's anemometer ran to 120 mph, and on other occasions he had seen it top out.

Gillespie showed up at 9 A.M., running up the rocky dirt path through the rain to get into the house as Allen's wife left for work. Huddling up in the living room, they felt that their world was under siege. "We were standing on this little island, this beautiful analog structure that Carver had designed at the top of the mountain" from which you could theoretically see the city in the distance, the froth of the ocean, the glow of San Francisco, the jeweled lights of Monterey—symbolizing huge potential markets for neuromorphic transducers and elegant neural networks. But at the time all you could actually see, feel, or hear were the gales of creative destruction winging up from Silicon Valley and Japan against the windows of the house.

Nonetheless, hunched over that kitchen counter of gray granite in the eight-faceted 180-degree curve of the living-room glass, they found an eye in the storm. Totally absorbed in the project, blocking out the world, they created a design for a workable touch pad based on Allen's concepts and on Gillespie's shrewd ways of squeezing the last bit of computation out of cheap eight-bit digital microcontrollers. They could do much of the calculation on special-purpose digital circuits on chips. But if you were going to move all the rest of the computing to the microcontroller, it had better be able to do the job in real time. "Dave did a brilliant job," said Allen, "of partitioning the algebra so the right answers dropped out naturally."

So it went. Again and again they chose to replace clever analog solutions beloved of Carver and even Federico with digital devices. As they worked through the lessons of previous projects, they found themselves shunting aside, one device at a time, most of the some thirty patented analog circuits that the company had concocted over the years.

For Allen and Gillespie, stalwart graduates of Carverland, this was painful. "Going to digital," as Allen put it, "was like deciding to leave home. To run away from your parents. But analog was too hard, too slow. It dragged me down into the details too quickly, slowed the rate of experimentation. In the end I couldn't stand it. So we began to simulate stuff in digital. It's just a simulation, right? Yeah, but it worked pretty well. It felt empowering." It was analog concepts that they were simulating. But everything in the real world is analog. All digital processes ape analog functions conducted by the mostly analog human brain. In this touch pad, there would be no analog floating gates, no electronic potentiometers, no clever analog adders and multipliers. A digital microcontroller from Microchip of Chandler, Arizona, would perform many of those computations.

Allen and Gillespie finished their work just as the storm

relented and the sun began to peer through the clouds and the image outside their window began to take shape from the murk. As they stood up and looked at each other, they at first were exultant. They had a design for survival as a company. But in electronics, as they knew, there were many designs, not many products, and most companies ultimately go broke. They were just two engineers in a very flat organization, and they lacked any clear channel to impose these last-minute ideas on their company.

Neither Allen nor Gillespie was used to company politics, and neither knew the next step. But whatever it was, it would mean a severe attack on the work of a colleague. As the senior figure Allen would have to do the job, and he had no such experience. Miller and Faggin were close, he knew, and Miller's design was well down the pipeline. The train had already left the station. It would not be easy to stop. With the heavy use of digital, moreover, Allen doubted he could gain Mead's support. "Mead's not going to like this," he said.

But Gillespie insisted, "You have got to have lunch with Carver."

Filled with trepidation, Allen arrived the next day at the Late for the Train restaurant on Middlefield Road in Menlo Park to have lunch with Mead. "I fully thought I was already too late. I was cruising for trouble."

"We have a problem at Synaptics," Allen said. He explained the problems with Bob Miller's touch pad and the digital-dependent solution he and Gillespie had crafted. Then he waited for Mead's reaction. After an excruciating pause, Mead finally spoke:

"It's an adaptive analog circuit doing collective computation. I like it a lot. I think you've grokked it, Tim."

Mead had immediately grasped the validity of the new design and endorsed it. He had been listening to the technology, and it was telling him what it had told his students—analog has a crucial place. But if you want to do a computation, buy a computer. He told Allen to work out the details in a memo and fax it to Faggin in Japan, where he was attending a conference. In the course of writing the memo, Mead says, Allen significantly improved the design.

Faggin was also ready for a new design. Unbeknownst to Allen and Gillespie, Faggin himself had become deeply suspicious of analog computation. By the time he arrived at Zanker Road, he was ready to put Allen in charge of the project and move Miller to a new role, managing relations with the contract manufacturers.

Then in May 1994 emerged the new Apple Powerbook, with its Cirque touch pad on four digital ASICs. It brought widespread acclaim as a major advance over trackballs. The PC industry immediately began to look for suppliers for a touch pad for PC-compatible notebooks. Alps was soon in the market with its own two-chip solution. In a critical decision, Faggin immediately resolved to adopt the Alps form factor, all the same connectors and power levels. He purchased drivers from the same contractor used by Alps.

Alps's device, however, suffered from sensitivity to ambient electromagnetism and moisture. Synaptics's pad did not. After the experiences with previous Synaptics products, Allen and Gillespie had incorporated on-chip error correction and redundancy and used redundant memory technology pioneered in mainframe computers. These decisions increased costs, but they also enhanced the immunity of the pad to outside interference. Allen and Gillespie chose one-time changeable EPROMs (erasable programmable read only memories) for the firmware over the significantly cheaper but unchangeable ROMs. All these decisions turned out to be crucial. When, three months later, the Synaptics touch pad was ready, it was precisely the device that the entire PC notebook computer industry was seeking. If a company wanted a slightly different device, however, the firmware could be altered.

"Timing is everything in this business," Faggin says. "Sometimes it helps just to be lucky." And it helped to be prepared. Full of analog-sensor and neural-network experts, Synaptics had been preparing for this moment for five years.

As Gillespie reflects, "Touch pads turned out to be not merely a good fit for the company's expertise, but a perfect fit. A touch pad converges a mass of ambiguous capacitive signals, and the answer you want is 'Where is the finger?' You put all this murky data into a pot, stir it around, and hope to get a solid dependable answer. By taking a bunch of crummy estimates and have them all vote you can get a very high quality response. It is not literally a neural network—it has no Hopfield algorithm, for example—but it is a similar kind of collective computation, trying to bridge the analog domain of messy real-world signals with the computer domain of digital precision."

With all the backing and filling and to-and-froing across the pad as it settled for the correct path, the processor had to perform a kind of cognitive annealing. Settling on a correct path for the company, it was finally time to plunge the Synaptics sword into the icy turbulence of the personal computer market. Over the next six months, with deceptive ease, the company managed to capture some 60 percent of the global touch-pad market. Holding most of the rest was Alps in Japan.

Then Logitech came forth with its own pad. Designed under Bisset's guidance, cultivated at Synaptics, it was a one-chip device. Synaptics was still using two chips, which in theory at least would be twice as expensive to manufacture. Logitech set the price of its system at $6.50, nearly 30 percent below Synaptics's price of $9.00. At $6.50, Synaptics would lose money on every pad it sold. The battle seemed to be over.

In the price war that followed, Logitech did make some small inroads into the market. But Allen and Gillespie were already intensely at work on a new single-chip solution incorporating all the advances of the two-chip system. Faggin put Gillespie in charge of the task of designing a microprocessor exactly customized for all the special demands of touch pads. Gillespie demurred. Designing a microprocessor is something that the titans of the industry—people like Federico—accomplish through legendary feats of genius and tenacity. But Faggin persuaded Gillespie that it did not take a "god or a Faggin to make a microprocessor."

With Gillespie leading the processor design and the firmware and Allen contriving the overall design, the one-chip solution emerged in 1997. At that time one of Logitech's main customers, the contract manufacturer of Compaq's notebook, came to Faggin to report problems with the Logitech device, which was sensitive to interference. Did they have an alternative? Faggin was ready to plunge in the sword again. With its error correction, adaptable EPROMs, and neural algorithms, the Synaptics product proved far more robust than any other touch pad. Within a year, Logitech was virtually out of the market, and in 1999 it withdrew entirely. "They threw in the sponge. We had it," said Faggin. Facing defectors from Synaptics, former partners at Logitech, a continual stream of analog frustrations, Faggin had finally triumphed in a new company with a radically new product. His vindication was sweet.

Meanwhile, amid all the excitement over the touch-pad breakthrough, few noticed that Carver and his team had taken a remarkable picture of a cat.

A scarcely visible cat lurks behind the blue pixels in the cover photo-graph for Carver Mead and Misha Mahowald's Scientific American *article on the future of analog imaging. Could this technology ever threaten Kodak?*

16

The Cat

While Faggin early in the 1990s was taking Synaptics on his happy ride into haptics—touch pads—Mead's imager projects remained far short of the market. But perhaps because they tapped a deeper stream of scientific research, they continued, ever so slowly, ever so relentlessly, to gather momentum both with Mead's little team at Synaptics and with Misha and her colleagues at Caltech.

Fruits of Mead's collaboration with Mahowald spanned the entire history of Synaptics, beginning a few months before its launch in 1986, when Misha was embarking on her career as a graduate student, through her departure to Europe in 1992, and through the power of her design ideas afterwards.

In 1987, in a Caltech classroom, Mead first publicly declared his conviction that what he termed "neuromorphic analog VLSI" offered the possibility of a radically more effective image processor. For Mead, this assertion was not new. But later in the class, he presented the first actual example of such a machine, a silicon retina chip, based on Misha's design. Modeled on the human eye, it could follow a rotating fan without aliasing (reversing direction as spinning wheels do in movies). It could also adapt to drastic changes in the intensity of light. The images it offered at the time were crude. But unlike all the other crude imagers of the time, including the popular digital imagers used in the robotics industry to inspect work in progress in factories, these images reflected a deep study of brain functions and processes.

Mead explained: "When you examine how biology processes visual information, several facts are clear. Even the brain of a fly as it eludes a swatter outperforms any real-time computer image system by as many as nine orders of magnitude [billions]." He meant that the "power delay product"—comparing the power usage with the processing speed—of the fly's neural reflex system is incomparably superior to anything computer science can build or even model. "We have almost no idea of how the fly does it. And if we cannot figure out how the fly does it, we do not know how the far more complex human brain does it."

The operation of the brain shares virtually nothing with a conventional digital computer. It is not serial and it does not have a separate memory. It does not have a glossary of symbols. Forced to work in real time—creatures with von Neuman imagers would have been eaten by creatures with real-time brains—the key neural constraints are energy and connections. The brain had to work in a remorseless environment of scarcity, in time, power, and communications.

Examining the brain, we find that unlike a computer

schematic, which is dominated by several layers of long-distance wire—adding up to some seven miles—the brain is supremely local. Less than 1 percent of its wires are remote. Less than 1 percent of its energy, which in turn is less than 1 percent of the 80 watts used in a leading-edge microprocessor, is devoted to transmitting signals between different parts of the brain. Although some experts have spoken of the "huge communications resources" of the brain, involving "millions" of axons (the long-distance links), these millions compare to local billions of millions of connections. The millions of axons represent roughly one-billionth of the total synaptic lines, which number on the order of quadrillions (10^{15}). The brain lavishes some 70 percent of its energy on dendritic processing, the input trees that link to the neurons. Though McCullough and other neural-network champions have termed this a passive process, this 70 percent figure implies an active and transformative kind of communication, resembling a data flow or systolic array more than a von Neumann computer.

Calculated in the 1980s by Margaret Wong Reilly of the University of Michigan, these percentages reflect the energy dynamics of the only image processor that demonstrably works. They overthrow all the prevailing assumptions of passive imager technology. "I do not imagine that I understand the brain in any full way," Mead says. "But our retina chip is based on what we do understand. The result is that it operates at least 10^4 times more efficiently than digital imagers do and it can simulate some of the functions of vision on silicon in real time."

It was a significant first step toward creating a real-time

imager on monolithic silicon. In the future, Mead believed, such silicon devices could empower improved forms of machine vision or superior solid-state cameras that could process images as well as merely take pictures.

To the argument that such an analog system would require exotic designs and thousands of discrete devices that would be too cumbersome to build, Mead offered his device in the plain bulk CMOS silicon used in all the digital chips in your PC. To the argument that it would use too much power, he ran CMOS transistors at exquisitely low power. Both the N (negative) electricity of electrons and P (positive) electricity of "holes" (where electrons were missing from the material) he ran at subthreshold voltages like the micropower systems in digital watches. Even the light-receiving photoreceptors needed no complicated addition to the CMOS process.

Every CMOS designer faces a fundamental problem. Between every cell's two transistors—the complementary negative and positive devices—is a potential bipolar transistor, called the latch-up or parasitic device. It can crop up across what is called a space charge region between the two CMOS transistors. Where positive and negative forces meet in a device is an active area termed a P/N junction: a scrimmage line where contend the negative electrons and the holes (electrons missing from the structure of an atom). Every CMOS process has to figure out some way to neutralize the potential parasite "latch-up" between the transistor that is switched by a positive voltage on its gate and the transistor that is switched by a negative voltage on its gate. But rather than neutralizing it, Mead listened to the technology, and actually enlarged and enhanced the bipolar latch-up transistor that the silicon wanted to provide. He made it into a combined photodetector and signal amplifier.

Collecting light on the P/N junction at its base, the latch-up transistor amplified the signal in the channel between its source and emitter. With gain of over 1,000, the latch-up outperformed ordinary photodiodes that would have to be placed on a separate chip from the image processor. Integrating the photodetectors onto the CMOS device, Mead showed the way to create analog systems that scaled like digital systems in accord with Moore's Law.

The latch-up photodetectors play the same essential roles as the 6 million cones and 120 million rods in the human eye. A single photon with an energy larger than the silicon band gap will create an electron-"hole" pair that causes swarms of electrons in the base of the transistor to cross the channel. Governing the amplifying gain of the transistor is the life span of the electron hole pairs—how many holes can pass through the base channel before they recombine with electrons and lose their charge. In this case, the transistor multiplies one photon into hundreds of electron charges. Similarly, in a human retina, a rod converts a single photon into a million electrons worth of charge in the form of sodium ions, with a gain dependent on their life span. Though radically different in detail, both are analog cascades of amplification that use the lapse of time as a crucial guide in generating an image.

The human eyes and mind see and sense by the analogies embodied in the neurochemistry and electrical patterns in the brain. They don't even know it's hard. By contrast, a high-resolution digital imager takes billions of steps every second and consumes scores of watts of power and heat to calculate a single picture.

Only with agonizing delays, however, would Mead's analog VLSI gain adherents outside the circle of his own students. Presenting his ideas to an audience at MIT a few months after his classroom revelation of the analog retina chip in 1986, I incurred unfriendly classroom guffaws and endured some of the resentment provoked by Mead's new insights. The MIT professors were proposing optical computers that used photonic devices modeled on digital transistors. They laughed out loud at my assertion, borrowed from Mead, that the absence of digital optics in the brain—the world's only fully successful image processor—cast serious doubt on the prospects for image processing with digital optics.

Only slowly did the analog retina chip crawl forward. But four years later, in May 1991, after between twenty and thirty iterations of the device in Carver's lab, it made the cover of *Scientific American*. Representing this technology to the world of science was the face of a cat registered by Mead and Mahowald's retinal camera. Inside, the story by Mead and Misha was confident: "The behavior of the artificial retina demonstrates the remarkable power of the analog computing paradigm embodied in neural circuits. . . . A neuron is an analog device: Its computations are based on smoothly varying ion currents rather than on bits representing discrete ones and zeros. Yet neural systems work with basic physics rather than trying constantly to work against it. . . ."

As Mahowald explains in her book, *An Analog VLSI System for Stereoscopic Vision*, "The analog system functions as part of the real, physical world, at the same level as the system [the retina] that it emulates. It interacts directly with the visual world. . . . [Its] responses are real-time electrical signals . . . measured much as are the signals in a real physiological preparation—with an oscilloscope. The similarities between the analog system and the biological one facilitate comparison between the two and create a milieu of serendipity."

Mahowald was expressing her delight with the similarities between analog electronics and biological processes. In contrast to the immediate translation of light signals into digital numbers to be crunched into an image, the analog and biological imagers shape the light into a cascade of related chemical and electrical radiations. They do not cut off nature and resort to mathematical abstractions. They use the amplified signals from the light and allow them to flow as a pattern across the neural plane.

The result, as Mead and Mahowald wrote in *Scientific American*, was huge energy efficiency: "In digital systems, data and computational operations must be converted into binary code, a process that requires about 10,000 digital voltage changes per operation. Analog devices carry out the same operation in one step and so decrease the power consumption of silicon circuits by a factor of about 10,000. . . ."

They pointed to a little recognized virtue of analog devices that would prove pivotal in the development of future imagers: "They respond to differences in signal amplitude rather than to absolute signal levels, thus largely eliminating the need for precise calibration. . . ." As Misha pointed out in her book, the eye only sees changes, or by changing. It detects the movement of objects or it sees still objects by constantly moving itself. While digital imagers are bolted down and treat movement as noise, movement is the key signal and guide for a biological imager. If the eyeball, for example, is frozen in one place, it becomes blind. It sees by moving and focuses on movement. Vision machines that try to remove the noise of movement defy the lessons of nature.

Misha concludes: "Because [in Claude Shannon's theory of information] only changes and differences convey information, constant change is a necessity for neural systems—rather than a source of difficulty, as it is for digital systems. . . . The success of this venture will give rise to an entirely new view of information processing that harnesses the power of analog collective systems to solve problems that are intractable by conventional digital methods."

All this was theory, however. Regardless of its academic significance as evidence of an advance in understanding the nature of vision, the cat on the cover—a monochrome blur in blue—actually was a downer for most observers. It belied both the confident assertions inside and the grandiose claims of the Synaptics's business plan. Captured in only 2,500 pixels, the image seemed to pose no significant threat to the Moore's Law juggernaut of digital electronics based on charge-coupled devices that was already propelling a thriving industry of machine vision for manufacturing applications. With a single "bucket brigade" CCD chip holding millions of pixels, many company laboratories were experimenting with digital cameras that offered resolutions far higher than Mead's. Few were awed by his claim that he could scale his device to densities a hundredfold greater than the early rendition. Some 250,000 monochrome pixels scarcely endangered Kodak or Sony.

17

Teleology at Oxford

fter Misha's *Scientific American* breakthrough and her thesis triumph, she left for Oxford, where she would confront the world of biology in its own lair. Unlike Carverland, congested with computers and oscilloscopes and other scientific instruments, the Oxford lab was filled with books and prowled by real cats. Her colleagues, Rodney Douglas and Kevan Martin, though pursuing the neuromorphic vision, were nervous about its implicit critique of biological practices.

As Misha put it at the time: "Biologists don't want to have a goal. They call that 'teleology' and think it's bad. They want to measure everything objectively, all the infinite details, without understanding the purpose. But in order to understand something, you have to take things out. If you want to understand a cat, here's a cat"—a black feline jumps onto the lap of her mind—"it's all there. Perfect." She holds out her cupped hands. "But to understand a cat, you must reduce it somehow. Make judgments. Have a goal.

"Making models of the retina with Carver, we have to take almost everything out that the biologists think is important. Take out the chemistry, the DNA, the shape, the salt water, the lipids. In making a silicon model, we take out everything but a few electronic properties that look the same—amazingly the same—as the biological properties and signal paths. But if you dump the chip in salt water it reacts differently. It will short out.

"The biologists do the same thing every time they do a measurement. They take everything out they don't measure. But they don't admit it. So they never develop a clear agenda and a set of goals for their research." Biologists at Oxford that year in fact were studying the neurons of live cats by probing them with a sensor that could measure their electrical activity on an oscilloscope. But these crude measures yielded little understanding and were very bad for the cats. Misha conceived vision as a complex collective feat of billions of neurons, rendering the blips of one neuron essentially meaningless. But at times she thought that even this bootless torture of cats offered more insight into the brain than her own efforts to create neurodes on silicon.

During the long winter in Oxford, she moved in with her colleague Rodney Douglas, a genial and accomplished English biologist and neuromorph, recently divorced. "I cannot separate my life from my work," she said. As time passed, though, the work bogged down and other biologists at Oxford outside their little group showed little interest or support. The team was exultant when ETH in Zurich established and endowed an entire new institute to support Misha's work and housed it in a spanking new building. It is called the Institute for Neuroinformatics.

In 1995, Misha and most of the group moved to Zurich, including Douglas, Martin, and a team of ten scientists. Their goal is familiar: "to identify the computational principles that make the brain so formidably versatile and powerful, and attempt to embody them into a new and innovative type of computer architecture." Their chief achievement is the "canonical cortical microcircuit," a kind of minimal electronic neurode that theoretically could be ganged into groups to perform neuromorphic computation.

MEANWHILE BACK IN San Jose, Mead was pursuing his imager project in a corner of the Synaptics Lab. In late 1994, impressed by claims of progress on the imagers, National Semiconductor—a Silicon Valley behemoth with some $2 billion in revenues—made a bid to buy Synaptics. The purchase did not go through because of resistance on the Synaptics side, but National made a $5 million investment. It put its COO Dick Sanquini on Synaptics's board of directors and agreed to pursue a joint development project, to be negotiated by the two companies. To Mead, this proposal offered the appealing chance to have ready access to a leading-edge fab. He suggested that the joint development be devoted to imagers.

In charge of the joint venture, Mead hired Tobi Delbrück to build the imagers and National assigned two engineers. They set up a lab at Synaptics where they contrived small cameras based on imaging chips that Mead and Delbrück had developed. Carver began having fun again because "we were doing fun stuff." But as time passed, he discovered that despite weekly Friday meetings with National executives and engineers, he lacked leverage with the National fab.

Mead was near the end of his rope when Mark Grant, in charge of National's patents, showed up at one of the Friday meetings in April 1996. After it was over, he approached Mead and asked him how it was going. Mead was seething at the time. He said he didn't know, because it was so hard to get National to put anything into silicon. Grant replied: "You know, Carver, that is not really the issue. We have cross-license agreements with all the other semiconductor companies. Any patents you come up with on imagers will be available to all the others. The only way your ideas will have any value is if they are spun out into a separate company."

Mead was exultant. Grant had given him a perfectly valid reason why National would benefit if the imager project became independent. The company would not want any of the new intellectual property being accumulated on Zanker Road to slip away to Intel and Sony or any other major microchip producer in the world.

The group was already developing the first CMOS imaging sensors. Using Mead's invention based on bipolar latch-up transistors that could be made into photodetectors in an ordinary silicon fab, they could achieve densities bounded only by the advance of CMOS technology. Doubling transistor densities every eighteen months under Moore's Law, the process was already scheduled to produce a billion-transistor DRAM early in the next century.

Next to be hired, in August 1996, was Nick Mascarenhas. A particle physicist who had joined Carver as a postdoctoral fellow, he had devoted much of his academic career to detecting neutrinos, massless particles that pervade the universe but interact with almost nothing, making them incredibly hard to catch. If he could detect neutrinos, photons should be a snap.

FROM THE OUTSET of the new independent imager project, Carver upheld two key principles. He knew that the company could not succeed making imagers alone. The Verifone experience had confirmed his resolution to avoid dependence on the whims of a large company. The imager joint venture would have to produce entire cameras, from shutter to software. Even if they never marketed a camera, they would need to build one in order to prove the capabilities of their imager. The second resolution was to create a color camera without arrays of filters each dedicated to just one color. Eschewing digital guesswork, the new camera would have to register *all* the colors at every pixel.

One day in September 1996 Mead showed up at the lab with an old tube-based video camera. It used a prism to separate the three colors of light for processing into a full-color image by three tubes. Carver suggested that they extract the tubes from the prism element and do a color imager with three imager chips, one for each color, attached to the prism. This design was cumbersome, but it possessed the supreme virtue of collecting all the light from all three primary colors at every pixel. By January 1997, Tobi Delbrück completed a working prototype, based on chips manufactured at National. It took him a little more than two months. It was the first camera they made. It produced clean and vivid images of 640 by 480 VGA resolution, like a cheap PC, or some 300,000 pixels. It was a start.

With a tiny team and few resources, they had demonstrated in two months the ability to make a camera with images of higher quality than the prevailing standard in digital photography in 1997. But they could not proceed further without support from National. The key event was a demo done by Mead, Toby Delbrück, and Nick Mascarenhas at a Friday meeting with National in April 1997. Assembled in a National boardroom were CEO Brian Halla, Dick Sanquini, and technical staff, including an imager and wafer fab expert named Dick Merrill. Tension was high. Delbrück and Mascarenhas had never seen Mead so nervy and focused. "Assembled with duct tape," the device consisted of a TV camera lens mounted on a single circuit board and attached to a computer color monitor. After it was set up, Mead told Tobi and Nick sharply, "Don't touch it."

The National executives all paraded by the machine and looked at themselves live in VGA color. With few defects or bad pixels, the device offered a clean image with good color saturation. Everyone seemed impressed, although Merrill was quiet. The high resolution, low noise, and high potential were evident. National began exploratory negotiations for a deal with Synaptics.

Mead then met with Sanquini and patent counsel Grant, and together they made a proposal: National would invest in a new company and put all their imager patents into it. Synaptics would also put in their intellectual property in imaging and assign key personnel, namely Mead, Delbrück, and Mascarenhas. Although those terms summed up the deal that was finally negotiated, Mead recalls: "The process took six months to close because once you get in the lawyers, they have to add value. The way they add value is to change the deal in such a way that it does not work anymore." But just as Mead was near to giving up hope, Sanquini called: "Isn't the problem that we are just not communicating? Let's have a another meeting, just you and me . . . and the key lawyers, of course." Mead gulped ("key lawyers, of course"), but he actually was pleased, because he knew exactly which lawyer to bring.

Sanquini came with Mark Clark, the National counsel, and Mead brought Craig Johnson of the Venture Law Group, the leading entrepreneurial lawyer in Silicon Valley, now also chairman of Garage Technology Ventures. Johnson is known throughout the Valley as a wizard at structuring win-win technology deals. As they began hammering out the agreement, he began talking reflectively about the structure of arrangements he had seen work and those that didn't. "The key for any good to come out is that the big companies leave the entrepreneurs and engineers room for independence." With Johnson's authoritative guidance, they made a deal that gave Mead and his team the space to innovate, and National and Synaptics a bountiful share of the upside. At the time National held 49 percent of the equity and Synaptics 16 percent.

Before launching the new company, however, Mead had to be sure of one thing. There were two people he knew he would have to sign up. One was Richard Lyon, former Caltech student and teacher, at the time resting on a gilded six-month severance package from Apple. The other was National's leading inventor of imagers and silicon processes, Dick Merrill. Merrill still was suspicious of Mead as a pointy-headed academic who did not understand quite how to design a device that worked well outside the hothouse environment of a Caltech laboratory. But Mead was quick to recognize Merrill as "the most creative engineer that I had ever met."

"He was extremely elusive, though," Mead said. And before the company could be consummated, Mead would first have to visit Misha in Switzerland.

18

White Rabbit

Sometimes I doubt the reality of a separate
consciousness. —Misha Mahowald

In September 1996, Carver Mead got a report that Misha
was in serious trouble in Zurich. She had moved out of Rodney Douglas's apartment and was living alone. She had not
been able to focus on her work. She needed "space." She needed
"time."

As everyone discovers, when they take brain science seriously,
it is a hard problem. Mead had modest goals of moving step-by-
step, like an engineer. Misha was more impatient. She wanted
bionic breakthroughs, psychedelic revelations. Beseiged by
murky data, dendritic loops within loops, neuronal mazes within
mazes, a susurrus of analog noise, a buzz of bugs and flies, howls
of dying cats bristling with metal probes, she felt trapped.

Seeking the doors of perception, she kept hitting the walls of
recursion. In confinement, no system can be fully understood.
No logical scheme, mathematical code, or algorithm can be
proven without resort to premises beyond itself. Kurt Gödel had
defined the problem. Max Delbrück had couched it in his Mun-

chausen epigram. Misha resorted to yoga. She resorted to animistic prayer. She even returned fitfully, but recurrently, to the forms and symbols of her original Catholic faith. She struggled to extract her mind from the swamp by pulling on her own long braid.

Like so many brain researchers before her, from Aldous Huxley to Timothy Leary, she had sought in her desperation a facile Disney-like epiphany, an artificial ride into the mind, and out into a higher domain. At first the drugs—particularly the LSD and THC—gave her a sense of new insight and power. But over the years they began to evoke frightening specters beyond her control. She then halted drug use entirely, to the extent of refusing even an enhanced form of aspirin offered her by Feinstein for a headache. But without drugs she found herself prone to depression. She had wanted to transcend her limits, enter a universal consciousness beyond the cerebral trap, look down on her own mind from a universal eye. But there, knowledge stops, phantoms fly, and demons lurk. Checkmate.

Mead and his companion, Barbara, flew to Switzerland to see her. Arriving at her apartment with flowers after a flight from California, they were greeted by Misha with a strangely cold and dismissive shrug, as if she were not really there and they were not really there, as if the world had receded and she were a waif, diminishing down a long tunnel, all Disney magic gone, and they were inspecting her from a microscope above. They did their best to reach her, without success.

In late December, Misha summoned David Feinstein to Geneva. Her old Caltech lover and most enduring friend and confidante, he had been the one who first contemplated her retinal map and grasped its promise. It was he who introduced her to Carver Mead. Although in 1992 she and David had amicably broken up to pursue their divergent careers, they had continued to talk weekly on the phone, Feinstein at Boeing in Seattle, Misha in Pasadena and Oxford. Feinstein came now to try a rescue.

Misha wanted him to arrive on Christmas morning, and so he did. There were St. Nicholas decorations everywhere. Bells ringing. Churches beckoning. Swiss burghers thronged the streets amid all the lights and consolations of the ordinary life that Misha had once wanted: love, family, children, revelation, God.

She greeted him bearing a King James Bible and restlessly shuffling rosary beads. Pointing to scripture, she told him she was being invaded by creatures crawling up from the base of her spine. They were beginning to prey on her mind. They were relentless. For distraction, she insisted on attending a Christmas carol party given by a friend from the institute. The songs were all in German. She did not seem to know anyone. Panic seized her. Feinstein called Rodney Douglas for advice. He assured him that this had happened before—that her medication would take effect in six hours and she would be okay. Ten hours later, while Feinstein lay sleeping in her living room, Misha left quietly.

Feinstein was awakened the next morning by policemen knocking on the door. Surveying the apartment, they opened the bathroom door. The tub was full and red with blood. On the floor was a ruddy kitchen knife. After an apparently unsuccessful attempt to cut her spinal chord, Misha had left the apartment for a nearby train station. She jumped in front of the train to Geneva. She was thirty-three years old.

FEINSTEIN WROTE TO Misha's friends: "Sometimes I find myself exclaiming, 'How could you do this, Misha?' But it isn't really a mystery. She was beset by demons within. She had a psychosis, and had come to believe that madness was coming to take her. She explained that if madness triumphed, then she would be eternally damned, whereas if she died by her own hand, then she might be redeemed. I hope she found redemption, however she conceived it."

Misha had told Feinstein of her conviction—contrived from scripture, imagination, figmentary recollections from her youth—that if she died before Christmas ended at the place of her birth in Minnesota, seven hours behind, she could find salvation. Otherwise the demons would capture her mind and she would be lost to madness and perdition. She did arrive at the station before six o'clock.

Feinstein continued: "I find Misha's story eerily like the story of Carl Jung. However, Jung's psychotic period in his thirties ended finally, releasing and empowering him to do his life's work.

"Misha was more connected to the collective subconscious than anyone I have ever known or known about, save perhaps Jung himself. That connection intensified abruptly during her 'long gray winter' in Oxford two and a half years ago and continued to deepen, increasingly threatening her sense of herself. My understanding of her death is that suicide became possible for her when her fear of loss of self surpassed her fear of death."

In 2000, Tim Allen went to visit his old friend Tom Tucker. At Caltech, Tucker was the incandescent one, as intellectually sparkling as was Misha, with whom he tested the doors of perception and the elasticities of the mind. Allen found Tucker living on his mother's couch in Littleton, Colorado. He had a blank expression and little to say.

FEINSTEIN WORKED AT Boeing for seven years as a technical leader on neural networks and then became chief scientist at a start-up called MicroMonitors that created liquid crystal displays. It failed during the millennial technology crash. Now he lives in a white house propped up on the side of the hill overlooking Portland, Oregon, with a no-nonsense young woman social worker, a huge dog, and several cats. On Thursdays, he teaches mathematics as a volunteer to troubled youths in prisons.

Through his company, Analytic Animations, he consults on the intractable problems of applied mathematics with companies around the globe. At a time when some scholars write of the end of science and assert that all the major problems are solved, the frontiers of human learning still beckon to Feinstein on all sides. He believes that "the horizons of knowledge are no more than a week away. Within a week of deeply delving into any field a smart researcher will reach its limits and begin asking questions that the leading thinkers in the field cannot answer."

Delivering "Feinsteins" of ever-increasing density and eloquence, he gives mesmerizing sermons before large crowds at local churches on the analogies between the findings of physics and the nature of the soul. "Waves are neither local (pin them down and they disappear) nor infinite (to propagate they need limits). But all the action happens at infinity." He believes that in some way Misha's waves flow on still.

Carver Mead, meanwhile, never solved the perplexities of the mind. But he did find a man who could bring Misha's retina project—however transformed—to a practical climax.

Part Four

FOVEON

19

Merrill's Magic

Walking through the Foveon Corporation parking lot with Dick Merrill on a cool February day in 2001, I did not know what to expect. Merrill is an *analog* chip designer, and analog people are different from digital people, who favor neat streams of ones and zeros and work in teams and earnestly entertain journalists. Analog people work at the physical layer, where everything is noisy and intimate and skewed and connected to everything else in the universe. This sense of exposure and connection—of a lack of thresholds and firewalls and the clear numerical boundaries of digital systems— makes analog people defensive. They often become loners, full of black arts and trade secrets, volatile resentments and spiky prejudices. One of the greatest, named Barrie Gilbert, has worked for some twenty-five years for Analog Devices of Norwood, Massachusetts, from a cabin somewhere in Oregon. Mead had met with Merrill four years before, in 1997, at the Lion & Compass Restaurant, not far from Foveon's offices, in an effort to enlist this silicon manufacturing sage in his new imager start-up. Mead was probably the most important intellect in the industry, and they were meeting in one of the elite eateries in the Valley. But Merrill had given the impression that he would rather be chomping on a ham-and-cheese sandwich in a cabin in Vermont.

FOR SEVERAL YEARS, Mead had urged me to meet with Merrill, whom he compares with the industry's most famously feral analog chip prodigy, the late legendary Robert Widlar. This was less than reassuring. As I researched *Microcosm*, my book on the semiconductor industry, for which I merely wished to make him a hero, Widlar had led me on a futile wild-geek chase from Lawrence Station in Sunnyvale to the Hilton in Puerto Vallarta, Mexico, without yielding a single interview.

On this bright Silicon Valley noon, Merrill seemed shifty, intense, and quiet, as if he was planning a Widlaresque getaway. But Merrill was at least unlikely to be drunk, or to flaunt a gun, or shoot it, as Widlar had been known to do, in efforts to attract the attention of his National Semiconductor bosses ("Always worked," as he said). And the trip to the Lion & Compass would be short. Merrill would not likely escape on the way. Mapquest estimated a seven-minute jaunt, just one exit down Route 101, which was only a few hundred yards up San Tomas Expressway from Foveon. But Merrill had a shortcut.

I steered my rental car, an ungainly gray Lincoln, out of the parking lot, squeezed across a small bridge and into a series of adjacent parking lots, snaking past the Intel Santa Clara plant and companies with names such as Swixx, Svee, and Luminant, onto what I thought was Central Expressway. Merrill was muttering directions and assured us it would be no time at all, what with the short cut, avoiding the jams and terrors of 101. Chiefly engaging Merrill, though, was his denunciation of the new Nikon D-1 digital camera. He had taken the top-of-the-line digital Nikon on a recent trip to Asia down the Mekong River with his Laotian wife, Sang. I was fascinated by this photography lecture. Using standard digital camera CCDs with all their noise, said Merrill, the Nikon was horribly flawed, inflicting ghastly whirls on the pictures where there should have been whorls, and forcing delays and wasting power (no ready plugs in Laos). "You only know you have a real camera when you want to take it mountain climbing," he explained.

After several turns, in the midst of a shameful capitulation toward Route 101 from Lawrence Expressway, Merrill announced that we had missed the key turnoff and overshot the mark. Turning onto a backstreet by a company sign with three Xs in it—whether adult or pre-IPO I could not descry—I suggested nervously that perhaps we should return to Foveon and eat in the cafeteria. "That will be fine for me," I reassured him. "I don't eat much lunch anyway." But Merrill still thought we could find the Lion & Compass any moment now, somewhere across 101 just off Magdalena, and we continued to thrash around for a total of some twenty-five minutes.

By the time we reached the restaurant, I knew enough not to buy a Nikon digital camera, but Merrill had still to explain how Foveon had arrived at its miraculous alternative.

By his shifty manner, Merrill conveyed the impression that

he really wished he could return to work and escape all these distractingly intimate questions about semiconductor P/N (positive/negative) junctions and charge-coupled devices. But right away, on arrival at the restaurant, he clarified Foveon's route to a revolution in image catchers. He said that our circuitous path to lunch offered a perfect analogy for the road that he, Mead, and his colleagues had followed on their way to their new imaging product.

Foveon and Synaptics had indeed traversed a twisting and swiveling route. They narrowly missed a possibly fatal collision with digital camera monster Sony. They overshot key turnoffs toward simple solutions. They pursued lengthy roundabout paths and kludges devoted to complex three-chip camera systems with exquisite precision optics and color supplied by epoxied prisms, all handcrafted, during the course of which the embattled team frequently debated whether they wanted to go to the destination anyway. Perhaps Foveon should have merely exploited the niche market of professional cameras that cost more than $70 thousand apiece. Selling them for half that amount would still be cheap tuition for a trip down the learning curve. Maybe in the end they could lease the things for a few thousand a month, like a T-1 line, and get as rich as Pacific Bell. . . .

IN THE LATE summer of 1997, preparing to launch Foveon, Mead also set out to recruit Dick Lyon, his old student, friend, teaching assistant, and a camera buff to boot. Inventor of the optical mouse, master of signal processing, and creator of retinas and cochleas at Caltech, Lyon was the kind of practical scientist who could bridge the realms of laboratory and production line, imager component and camera system. Mead had to have him aboard. Living on his golden severance from Apple, he readily succumbed to Carver's invitation. More challenging was Merrill, with his secure and lucrative role at National Semiconductor.

As much as Merrill valued his National position, he was more intrigued with the chance to launch new imagers himself. But at the historic lunch with Mead at the Lion & Compass, he still harbored suspicions toward these Caltech types. He knew Mead was a great guy, but he feared that he might have undue pride of authorship for his inventions and excess loyalty to the Caltech crowd and their sometimes figmentary artifacts of laboratory science. "He wanted to make sure we were going to do it right," Mead said. By the end of the lunch, Mead had persuaded him that despite forty years teaching physics, computation, and electrical engineering at Caltech, he knew something about designing for mass production too. He also agreed that Merrill would become technical leader of the effort.

When Merrill decided to join, Mead knew he had his company on the road. On August 7, 1997, the imager effort moved out of the increasingly cramped and busy Synaptics facility on Zanker Road and into new offices on Bubb Road in Cupertino. Arriving on August 7, Mead took along Delbrück, Mascarenhas, and Orion Pritchard from the Synaptics imager project and signed up two more National engineers: Rich Turner, who later became Foveon's VP of engineering, and layout master Milton Dong.

Responsible for all the manufacturing of chips, Merrill had

one major concern as he joined the company, namely those bipolar phototransistors. Already latent between every two transistors in every CMOS device, the bipolar transistor photodetector was a beautiful idea, with the virtue of supreme elegance and compactness. Crammed between the two ordinary CMOS transistors, it enabled dense retinas at a time when CMOS transistors alone still had feature sizes far too big for a high-resolution imager. Pushing the technology for two years, Delbrück and Mascarenhas would exploit its efficiency to create imagers with a full nine million pixels in 1997. Still beyond the reach of most digital cameras eight years later, it was a dazzling feat of circuit design. But, as both Delbrück and Merrill knew, for future applications it had fatal flaws.

CMOS geometries by the mid-1990s had dropped below a half micron. This was around the wavelength of visible light itself. With Moore's Law taking care of density, the new imperative was ease of manufacture. Creating bipolar phototransistors with consistent behavior in the midst of an industry standard CMOS process was going to be a bear, Merrill thought. At the least, it would require risky process changes that the National fab teams would resist.

A more crippling problem of the bipolar transistor was image lag. Because it was part of the CMOS pixel, the bipolar device worked like the eye: It had no hard reset. This meant that each subsequent frame was haunted by a brief ghost from the previous one. Though perfectly acceptable for a still camera, image lag would be a showstopper for the hybrid still and motion camera that Mead had targeted from the beginning.

Merrill knew that in order to displace Mead's elegant but tricky bipolar transistor, he would have to prove the superiority of a design of his own. Just two months after the founding of the company, he delivered. Merrill came into the weekly Monday meeting with test data from a new imager—the 3-T—that he had gotten back from the National fab two weeks before. Based on a photodetector design that could be instantly reset after each exposure, it provided a 2K by 2K, four-megapixel imager, with low noise, no image lag, and dual still and motion capabilities. "Merrill showed us it was a lot better than what I had come up with," said Mead. "It was time to bet the company on Merrill . . . for the first time."

Mead resolved to use the 3-T to make a professional high-end studio camera with a prism that directed light to three separate image sensors. Saving all the light at every pixel rather than filtering out two of the colors, this system would eventually outperform all other digital cameras in color accuracy and luminosity.

But this goal would be achieved only after some arduous color science from Dick Lyon.

20

Lyon's Den
of Many Colors

At the heart of the headquarters of Foveon Corporation are two emblematic spaces, reflecting the two different paths to the future pursued by the company's chief technologist, Dick Merrill, and its chief scientist, Dick Lyon.

Dick Merrill's space evokes his time-travel trappings. Gleaming in the middle is the aluminum chassis for the rasterfarian test gear that he attaches like an electrified dreadlock wig of wires and lasers to the pins and sockets of his little imager chips—applying merciless tortures until they confess every alias and aberration, pixel-leak and pico-capacitance, drift and jitter of their photoelectric behavior. (Hey, it all matters—this is analog.)

Dick Lyon's space, by contrast, is a library. Occupying one dim corner of the second floor, it offers plush chairs, reading lamps, photographic relics, esoteric slide rules, and archaic cameras surrounded on four sides with a total of some five hundred books—shiny new books with jackets, moldy old books with fraying backs, tall photography catalogs full of black-and-white and color images. The titles range from canonical works by James Clerk Maxwell and Hermann Helmholtz to some five editions of Robert William Graham (RWG, to you) Hunt's classic, *Reproduction of Color.* The shelves bulge with several MIT *Handbooks of Colorimetry* and an array of Kodachrome manuals and stacks of handbooks for Kodak Ektachrome development procedures E-3 through E-6. Discreetly horned into the corner of a bottom row is a copy of *Roundup* 1970, the El Paso yearbook that memorializes Lyon's third camera and his promise of a stunner of a fourth.

Both of these emblematic displays are dead serious, as is Foveon itself. Merrill's ability to extort detailed performance data from every device has been critical to the fast progress of the company as it constantly experiments with the new designs and circuitry that he concocts. Lyon, meanwhile, actually read most of those books, and his knowledge of their contents—every labyrinthine rune and wrinkle in the often cryptic lore of color science—was crucial to transforming Foveon from an innovative imager consultant, like Fill Factory in Holland, into a possible supplier of comprehensive camera and imaging solutions, hardware and software, like Kodak of old.

So let us retreat to Lyon's den and curl up with an exciting treatise on color theory . . .

Technically referring to a set of electromagnetic wavelengths or frequencies, the word *color* tempts physicists and engineers to imagine that they understand it, when they have barely a glint. Running from infrared through visible light to ultraviolet, with ever shorter wavelengths and higher frequencies, the spectrum of "colors" climbs a rising slope of energies (the formula for electromagnetic energy is the frequency times Planck's constant). Thus the frequency of a color is proportional to its energy.

The confusion arises in relation to "brightness"—the property of an image most striking to humans. Frequency only vaguely relates to brightness. In physics, brightness signifies the number of photons arriving per second, while frequency measures the number of waves per second in each one of those photons. All the regnant imagers in the industry—all the CCDs and CMOS photo-sensors—measure physical brightness, photons per second. But no imager can restrict itself to basic physics. Even if it gauges energies as well as intensities, it will produce graphic gibberish without any "colors" that humans will deem accurate.

To build a useful camera entails entering Mishaland and acquiring a mortifying knowledge of "wetware"—biology. You have to master not only the physical spectrum of frequencies but also the sensitivity spectrum of human eyes. Divided into long, medium, and short receptors (LMS curves) for "red," "green," and "blue," the six million cones of the human eye will detect zero "brightness" in radiant infrared, zero "brightness" in sizzling ultraviolet, and a peak of brightness at around the 500-nanometer wavelength of yellowish green on a forsythia bush. Human eyes will see different materials as the same color in some lights and as different colors in other lights. Things that are objectively and spectrally different such as dollar bills and maple leaves seem to be the same color. Heck, they *are* the same color.

Called metamerism, these common anomalies pose baffling problems to anyone who wishes to reduce photography to mere photo-detection. Things that look red to the human do not have to look red to the camera. Digital processing can adjust the hue as long as the camera and the eye both register the same color. But no amount of digital processing can correct for an imager that reports as different two items that the eye sees as the same, or reports as the same what the eye sees as different. The eye and the camera must err in the same way or you have less an image than a splash of expressionist art.

At its photoreceptors, an eye or an imager receives a mad lightspeed rush of unfiltered frequencies, reflected off, refracted through, and diffracted around objects in its ken, traveling diverse distances through the atmosphere in different phases, illuminated by sunlight, fluorescence, tungsten bulbs, lasers, stars, and candles and bearing no obvious signs or signatures. Taking this nearly infinite dimensional space of electromagnetic radiation and reducing it to the three dimensions of primary colors is the crucial first step in designing an imager.

"How that step is performed," as Lyon observes, "fixes it for all time. You can't undo that. You can't get it back." All the king's MIPS and all the king's DSPs cannot retrieve the colors in a scene once they have been inaccurately represented. Then once you have the primary colors, you have to adapt them to your display technology and to human spectral sensitivities by applying the right coefficients in a process called matrixing. When Merrill invents a new device for registering pixel values, Lyon must then do the work to adapt them to humans. At Foveon, this translation did not always go well.

ARRIVING AT THE new offices with Carver Mead and Orion Pritchard, on August 7, 1997, Lyon had no clear guidance on what his role as chief scientist would be. At first "chief scientist" seemed to mean janitorial aide, setting up desks and chairs, computers and white boards. After the setup was done, Lyon poked around awhile, looking for dusty areas in shadows of ignorance behind all the shiny Ph.D.s.

On first glance, knowledge abounded. At Foveon there would soon gather experts on the neutrino, authorities on retinal design, masters of microchip layout and fabrication, and in Carver Mead himself there was a polymathic repository of information on everything from quantum tunneling, VLSI circuitry, and image representation to the esthetics of power-line insulators, the enigmas of neuronal and dendritic processing, the topologies of computer systems, and the husbandry of hazelnuts at his farm in Oregon. One thing he didn't know much about was color science, beyond the theory of the physics. But he nudged Lyon toward the canonical book by R. W. G. Hunt, *Reproduction of Color*, saying: "Why don't you look at this?" Lyon soon figured out that the path to his fourth camera would run through the thickets of this science of color.

As he began, the first challenge was the endless prism crisis. Like everything that happened to Foveon, it was nearly fatal and nicely fortuitous. It turned out that projection prisms of the sort that Carver brought to the company from National Semiconductor were all but useless for color accuracy. As Lyon shortly discovered in the pages of R. W. G. Hunt, prism colors are asymmetrical. If a prism projects accurate colors, it will receive distorted colors. But their supplier—Optical Coatings Laboratory, Inc. (OCLI)—was first entranced with the idea of using projection prisms to usurp the cathode ray tube in billions of computer displays and then with the better idea of using prisms to separate infrared wavelengths in wavelength division multiplexing (WDM) optical systems for JDSU, the leading optical modules company. Why would anyone want a receiver prism for *visible* colors anyway? They weren't interested in making *that*.

Then Delbrück tore apart a camcorder and extracted a solid-state prism from it. But as the supplier of that prism, Collimated Holes Corp., pointed out with alarm, "That is an IBM prism—patented by IBM—can't use that." Lyon investigated and found that IBM had patented it for projection only, which would not bar Foveon from using it as a receiver. So they proceeded. In the end, the Foveon prisms would evolve into "a color-separating, beam-splitting prism assembly" made of five pieces of glass, including two "dichroic" mirrors that divide light into two frequencies. The contraption could be fabricated only with the help of a glass company in Russia and then could be incorporated into a camera only through an exquisitely exacting craft involving epoxy and picomotors that could pick and place imagers with submicron precision in three directions for gluing onto the prisms.

When all that work was done, you still had three streams of light that could be rendered as fully authentic colors only with the help of ingenious software from Lyon that merged a glint of violet into the red. That was a patent, and it led to world-beating color accuracy, but it made the manufacturing challenge even harder. Any error got manifested as a purple fringe. In the end, they achieved some of the most accurate colors and most expensive cameras in the industry—great cameras, endorsed by Hasselblad, buying in and briefly branding them. But for two years Hasselblad, despite increasingly harried visits from Mead, could not get its lenses in line. Making a few hundred units itself, Foveon became an exotic niche supplier of $50,000 cameras, which was not what Mead had in mind as a serious market. Beyond the near-perfect colors, the chief appeal of the instrument was to studio photographers who could triple their output by avoiding the time-consuming hassle of Polaroid first takes.

While Lyon juggled the hues of the prism camera, he continued to push on through his reading agenda. He scoured the books of color science. He pored through the ever-increasing piles of proposed inventions and other ideas from Merrill. One day he stumbled onto Merrill's old concept of a vertical color filter based on the wavelength-dependent absorbency of silicon. "I didn't know about this," he told Merrill. "Will it work for a camera?"

"I doubt it," Merrill said. "It is a real physical effect, but it is hard to make good colors out of it. The colors tend to merge together. Ask Carver."

Lyon went to Mead, who referred him to a paper written by Delbrück reporting on their previous experiments with the idea. The results were lousy. The colors smeared into a delta of mud. Lyon was discouraged. Beyond the exotic prisms, Foveon seemed to be running out of options. Would this be another episode from the Synaptics story—ingenious analog technology ultimately dwindling into an academic stunt?

Then Lyon began to scrutinize Mead's and Delbrück's data more closely. He noticed that they had tested the colors one depth at a time. The result was that the junction would collect charge from nearly all of whatever color light was focused on it. But Lyon speculated that the results might be different using a stack of three junctions at once. Competing for the light, the three junctions should divide it in accord with the principle of wavelength-dependent absorption depth. More of the high-energy blue should gather in the junction closest to the surface, while the green and red would sink a micron or so down. He asked Merrill to test this proposition.

In a process that took six weeks, Merrill managed to design a workable test pixel and run it through the National fab. Then he inserted it into his torture chamber. The outcome was still murky, but the telltale pattern of absorption depths was detectable. At least it offered more promise than the Mead-Delbrück results. Merrill thought he might be able to tweak it to separate the colors more.

Before Merrill accomplished the superior separation, Lyon resorted to his Mathworks program to combine the relevant data—the three stacked junctions in Merrill's pixel and the spectral sensitivities of actual human eyes. Correlating the differential capture of the three electronic junctions with the differential responses of the long, medium, and short cones in the retina, he noted that the error—the difference between the two curves—was below 10 percent. The Merrill mix and the retinal mix were both messy, but they were the same essential mess. The neat Kodachrome separations that they were trying to imitate were nice for projections—and the rich saturated colors of slides—but strikingly different from the curves of human vision. Lyon recalls: "Everyone looked at Merrill's results and said, 'You can't make a camera with that.' I looked at Merrill's results and said I could make a better camera with that than I could with a prism. I could make a better camera with that than I could with film."

This finding, if true, promised a supreme fulfillment of Mead's career-long romance with silicon and its properties. Silicon had become the perfect substrate for computation—and you got the PC. Silicon had become the perfect channel for light, and you got fiber optics. Now Lyon was opening the way to an ideal silicon single-chip imager. Using the physics of the material, one silicon sliver some five microns thick could perform all the feats of photodetection and color separation performed in other systems by at least three chips plus millions of tiny color filters that blocked out two thirds of the light at every pixel, plus a "blur" filter to smear out borderline errors, all coupled with digital signal processors to retrieve the lost colors by guesswork. Lyon graphed his results and showed them to Mead. For the first time, Mead believed that Foveon was near a single-chip color imager. The silicon camera was declared feasible.

Then in March 2000, Foveon received a call from on high. Intrigued by the color accuracy of the prism camera, Kodak in Rochester summoned the Foveon team to the bleak gray reaches of upstate New York to discuss its innovations. It was the moment they had been waiting for. Mead, Lyon, and engineering chief Rich Turner flew east and arrived in Rochester. After explaining to the Kodak engineers the advantages of the prism technology, Mead said they had a still-better idea on the way. He showed them the new Merrill chip, with its still-murky colors, and promised to make it much better. "Merrill is working on it now," he said. "This is the future of photography." The Kodak people laughed and then said, "Call us back when you can make pictures like these prism photos with it."

"But then it will be too late," said Mead. "Some other company will license it." Kodak was unimpressed by the threat. As the meeting deteriorated, Foveon's Rich Turner offered yet another of Merrill's ideas. National had just completed the conversion of its Portland, Maine, fab to the .18 micron industry state of the art. Extrapolating how many more pixels the smaller geometries would enable him to put on the Foveon black-and-white imager, Merrill calculated he could make a 16-million pixel device on one chip, far ahead of the rest of the industry then maxing out at around 4 megapixels. Perhaps Kodak would be interested in leading the industry to 16-megapixel imaging. Again, the Rochester colossus was unwilling to buy a license for a technology that did not yet exist. But they were impressed by Foveon's assurance.

When Mead heard the idea, he was also impressed, and urged Foveon itself to create this awesome 16-megapixel product.

"Why do you want to make something with no market? No customer need. There is no camera that can use it," one of the Foveon marketing executives protested.

"That has never stopped us in the past," Mead said. "If we can build the world's best photon catcher, the world will beat a path to our door."

A month later, Mead's decision began to bear fruit, when the company got a call from a Greg Gorman of Los Angeles. Who's he? was the general response. "Just one of the world's most acclaimed portraitists," said Foveon's marketing chief, Eric Zarakov. "He's got great shots of such stars as Leonardo diCaprio and Sharon Stone . . . Richard Gere . . . Kim Basinger . . . Drew Barrymore. Heck, Arnold Schwarzenegger. Who do you want?" An old friend of Foveon sales chief Larry Stevenson, Gorman was "always ready for something new—particularly if it was in black and white" (90 percent of his work was in black and white), and he had a male model ready in San Francisco.

In the photo journal *Eyestorm*, Zarakov read that Gorman's more informal pictures ranged from "intimate glances of the Hollywood demimonde to a sweaty Jeff Koons, sitting on the toilet, flanked by two leather-clad strumpets."

"Just imagine how they would look with Foveon," Zarakov said.

"But what are we supposed to do with this guy this afternoon?" asked Turner. "He's already seen our prism camera."

"Get on the stick and show him that 16-megapixel camera you

were playing with the other day. You know, photographing the map of the U.S. and zooming in so you could see every fiber in the paper it's printed on."

"Hey, that's not a camera!" Turner protested with a note of desperation. "That's just a prototype chip. The images are enhanced through a Photoshop hack." But Gorman had tried the prism camera and found that it produced files wonderfully free of noise, "like a perfect negative." Now he wanted to try this new Foveon chip he had heard about that could produce the world's highest-resolution black-and-white images. When?

"Well, he's already on the plane from L.A.," sales chief Stevenson interjected. "From there he goes to his house in Mendocino and then to Europe. This is the only day he's got."

"You guys are crazy," said Turner. But he and Dick Lyon rigged up the 16-megapixel chip on a breadboard and created a crude camera using the chassis from the prism product, with a filter attached on a cardboard cylinder. When Gorman appeared at the door, they tried to interest him in new refinements of the prism camera, but he said he knew all about that. He'd come to see the 16-megapixel black-and-white imager. "We've got a few chips," Lyon confessed, "But it isn't in a camera. No one has ever made a picture with it."

"I want to use that," Gorman said. "I want to take the world's first 16-megapixel picture." They set up the new "camera" contraption in the old prism studio. The model donned a cowboy hat, unbuttoned his shirt, and assumed a brooding pose of a Rodin "thinker." Gorman was thrilled. But when Turner looked at the electronic viewfinder, he saw nothing there. The scene was apparently fuzzed out by infrared radiation from the smoldering model. While Gorman looked on with a bemused expression, Turner taped a further filter onto the cardboard cylinder, which removed more of the light. Finally, with Turner handling the chassis and Gorman triggering the shutter and a strobe light, they took a series of portraits.

Turning over the raw files to Lyon, Turner had low expectations. But over the next three days, Lyon extracted from the some 20 megabytes of monochrome information one of Gorman's best portraits, a riveting black-and-white image of the model, with amazingly sharp definition and vivid detail. Lyon blew up the image to a lifesize photo eight feet high with no perceptible degradation even when viewed from inches away. Vitality shone from the model's features, bringing to mind a classic photo of actor James Dean from the movie *Giant* and recalling "Pope of Trash" director John Waters's comment: "Greg Gorman is the only person I'd let photograph my corpse."

It was indeed a historic picture, offering denser black-and-white pixels than ever before in a digital image. Beyond that one photo extracted by Lyon's alchemy, however, Foveon had nothing more to offer Gorman. A fervent devotee of leading-edge Canon cameras, he ended his trip at his studio in L.A. and did not return to Foveon. The early years at the company seemed to be repeating the pattern of the early years at Synaptics: great laboratory stunts and scientific advances but no marketable products. Foveon had no color system beyond the prisms and no market for a 16-megapixel black-and-white imager.

Meanwhile, there would surely be a market for a one-chip

color imager. But the more work Lyon lavished on the color effects of the device from Merrill, the less he found he could improve it, and it was nowhere near good enough. Perhaps the Kodak people had a point. Lyon had miscalculated the interplay of the silicon physics with the particular parameters of the CMOS fab process. Silicon might make a great color imager in theory, but there was no silicon semiconductor process that could yield an effective camera chip. Perhaps that was the reason that Kodak, Fuji, Canon, and Nikon had all previously patented the one-chip vertical imager and then abandoned it. The CMOS process entailed crucial steps that nullified the advantages of the material as a vertical filter. It was a showstopper. As they approached the key industry exposition, Photokina, in Cologne, Germany, in late September 2000, they still had no color process to sell but prism cameras, and there was a smaller market for them even than for exotic black-and-white imagers.

Then Dick Merrill emerged from his aluminum cave with another idea.

21

Photokina 2000 and Beyond

In a huge industry such as cameras, rare are the occasions that a new company like Foveon can arrest the attention of the relevant world of experts, media, and rival engineers. Held every two years in the vast reaches of the KölnMesse in Cologne, Germany, with total floor space 800 meters long and several hundred meters deep, with tens of thousands of exhibitors and hundreds of thousands of visitors, including five thousand from the media, Photokina is Comdex for cameras, the most intense commercial showcase and crucible in photography. Every company, every shutterbug and photo-bird on the planet, it seems, is there and on stage, testing the *son et lumière*, touting prototypes and photo-types, waving his arms and amplitudes, swinging her hips and chips, flashing her bulbs, and zooming his lenses, in front of towering multistoried exhibits shaped like cameras.

As Photokina 2000 approached—scheduled for late in September—Foveon had impressed people like Greg Gorman as some kind of technical leader with its prismatic contraptions, but you wouldn't want to commit your career to one of their cameras. And Foveon had nothing else to sell. When September passed, it would be a full two years before the industry would again gather in such frenzied force.

Nonetheless, just one month before Photokina 2000, while the company was still preparing to push its prisms to a mostly indifferent camera market, Dick Merrill emerged from his aluminum chassis with yet another concept for a single-chip color filter. Added to his original idea was a simple but revolutionary process step entirely compatible with the CMOS process flow. Still a company secret today, the new Merrill scheme turned the showstopper inside out. What had previously been an impossible obstacle to a vertical filter became a radical simplification and improvement. An invention as elegant as Carver Mead's exploitation of the parasitic bipolar transistor as a photodetector, Merrill's idea was still more commercially promising.

"But you can't do that," said Lyon. "That's crazy. No one has been able to do it before."

"Don't tell me what I can't do," said Merrill., "I've already done a lot of stuff like it."

"Well, if you can," said Lyon. "It sure would work."

Merrill had made a basic invention to render the X3 possible in an existing CMOS process. The output of the chip would change. There were many imponderables. In essense, the company would have to put its faith in Merrill's magic in the fab.

Even some of Foveon's own executives were doubtful. At just that time in late 2000, Jim Lau, the hero of Synaptics touch-pad manufacturing in Asia, came aboard as the new CEO, replacing Ray de Moulin, a former Kodak VP for professional cameras. After a nearly fifty-year career in the industry, de Moulin had announced a well-earned retirement. By following de Moulin, the master of high-end professional photography, with an expert on low-end manufacturing, Foveon signaled readiness to move in new directions. But what directions? Mead recalled: "Jim was all set to go off and make a more automated version of the prism camera. I said that by the time you get that to happen we will have the vertical colors working." Having seen the first messy chip results—and heard of the Kodak rejection—Lau was amazed that Mead and Merrill could see anything there. But for experienced silicon sages such as Mead and Merrill the murky prototype was no cause for dismay at all.

NEARLY EVERY EXPERIMENT in electronics starts within a shroud of noise, a mass of overlapping curves and spiky anomalies. Only with long experience can the engineer nurse forth the signal—the meaningful result—from the froth of "dark currents" and amplifier distortions and electromagnetic skews and environmental fuzz. The prototype that Merrill got from National's Advanced Techology Group fab in Santa Clara late in 2000 produced data in no obvious way better than the output of his two previous vertical pixel designs. But looking at the results, apparently a swamp of noise mixed with a turbid chromatic overlay, Merrill was pleased. Scrutinizing the mountain ranges of arrayed curves on the oscilloscope, the summer storms, and electrical turbulence, he could descry a workable retina. The mountains, they could be laid low, one at a time; the storms could be tamed, step-by-step; and the valleys raised up, oh, so delicately; and above the wilderness could arise a rainbow of perfect colors. Merrill was a past master at this process, and so was Mead. Doing his own calculations "so I could grasp what was really going on in the physics," he was also convinced that the new approach would work.

"WE BET THE company on Merrill" was Mead's refrain. "He knows when something is going to work. It's in his bones. Goes off and doesn't talk to anybody, and then some run of wafers will come back from the fab and it will have his little test chip. He'll hook it up in his lab to some twenty testers and come back with the data. And you know it's right."

AS PHOTOKINA APPROACHED, the big story came from Foveon's friends in Rochester. Kodak announced that they had created a 16-megapixel CCD imager, the world's first, best, and largest, and had incorporated it into a new $20,000 mosaic camera called the Pro-Back. At first, Mead and Lyon feared that Kodak had stolen Foveon's thunder. But in fact Kodak had put Foveon on the map, by defining the focal feat of the year.

By the time Photokina opened in Cologne on September 23, 2000, the only actual image from a 16-megapixel chip loomed over the front of the Foveon exhibit area. It was Greg Gorman's incandescent black-and-white picture of the cowboy model. An eight-foot-high image that revealed no distortion when scrutinized one foot away, it visibly announced a major breakthrough from the tiny new company.

Imager experts quickly calculated that Kodak's CCD was a monster device that would cost some $7,000 apiece, suitable only for the most costly cameras like the Pro-Back, while Foveon's CMOS chip was one quarter the size and could be produced in volume for under $300. Massively vindicating Mead's decision to make the 16-megapixel device was a huge flood of visitors to Foveon's display area.

Mead had contrived a gigantic game of mega—bait and switch. The people came to see the 16-megapixel imager and to be photographed by the high-resolution prism cameras, and de Moulin, formerly chief of professional photography at Kodak, was still there to push the advantages of prisms to all comers. But any serious inquirer was steered to a room in back, where Mead, Lyon, and Turner pitched a new single-chip color imager that existed chiefly in their minds and hearts and in the hands of Dick Merrill back in Santa Clara.

One of these serious inquirers was Michihiro Yamaki of Sigma in Japan. Compared to Canon or Nikon, Sigma was a relatively small company with fewer than one thousand employees and revenues of $140 million. It had previously specialized in lenses. But the ostensibly shy, dapper Yamaki harbored higher ambitions. He wanted to break out of Sigma's niche and build a major camera company. When he heard of the 16-megapixel CMOS imager, he insisted on visiting the Foveon exhibit.

Conceding that Foveon did not yet possess a 16-megapixel camera, Mead steered Yamaki into a back room to show him the X3 prototype, which was even farther from realization. It was smoke and mirrors and a sprite of silicon. But unlike the Kodak team in Rochester, Yamaki and his engineers immediately saw the significance of the X3 design and trusted Mead's assurance that it could soon be built. Before the end of the day, Mead and Yamaki shook hands on an agreement to launch a joint effort to create the first commercial camera based on the Foveon vertical filter. Sigma would do the mechanical camera design with exposure and ISO controls and would create the lenses, with the single-lens-reflex features that allow you to preview the image through the same lens that captures the picture. Foveon would do the imager hardware and software, the readout process, the display preparation, and the file-saving code. From chip design to software and file storage for an entirely new kind of camera, the two companies faced an awesome challenge.

DOWN THE HALL from Merrill's office at Foveon is what appears to be a heap of colorful Navajo blankets, with a sheet of glass resting on the top. Only when you try to remove the glass do you realize that it is a photograph, utterly indistinguishable in hue and fiber from the pile below it. Fooled by this device, you can understand Merrill's impatience with his mere Nikon in Laos. But this trompe l'oeil trick, done with prisms, is designed only to grab your eye, not to grab the entire imager market.

On the wall as you enter the Foveon building is a more significant photograph, one with a story that portends likely success in the company's imperial quest. Taken by Merrill in the spring of 2001, it depicts a vividly colorful totem pole in Vancouver, Washington, shot against a perfect blue sky. Sky, Merrill points out, offers the best visible index of the noise level in an imager. In Merrill's picture, the sky is impeccably blue. In the normal course of events in the silicon business, a new chip based on an original design and a novel manufacturing process goes through scores of iterations before it works the way its designers hoped. Many never do. But this impeccable image was the first product of the very first single-chip camera, which itself was based on the very first chip to emerge, under Merrill's direction, from the first full run at the National Semiconductor wafer fabrication plant in Portland, Maine.

Thus, Foveon's revolution begins to take shape. Yes, the totem pole picture is flawless, with exquisitely authentic hues and supreme resolution. But more crucially, it is the first working photograph made with a single-chip, full-color imager. The Foveon camera is no mere "digital camera," full of chips and microprocessors and mirrors and shutters—it is a fully solid-state machine, based around a single analog chip and virtually no mechanical paraphernalia, capable (like the human retina) of both still and moving images.

Single chips have a singular virtue: They can eventually be manufactured in volume at a cost as low as 80 cents a piece—about the price of the packaging. In other words, Foveon's X3, as the marketers have dubbed it—for "times three," signifying three colors at each pixel—will make possible throwaway cameras and surveillance devices with a resolution and accuracy approaching today's most costly Hasselblad. Merrill simply plugged his new microchip into a circuit board, installed the board in an old-fashioned nineteenth-century camera chassis, snapped the picture, and potentially transfigured an industry.

Between the invention and the marketplace, however, lies a long shadowy slough: a treacherous competitive realm, where dragons lurk.

Clayton Christensen, author of The Innovator's Dilemma, *issues a portentous challenge to Foveon: "Foveon cannot make cameras. It will lose."* Glenn Davis

22

Foveon's Disruptive Challenge

G reg Gorman had long held out as an advocate of film in a world moving to digital cameras and then long persisted as a champion of black-and-white images in a Hollywood scene garish with color. But in early 2003, this virtuoso photographer finally found an electronic camera that satisfied his exacting demands.

Although confessing that "I still love shooting my own black-and-white images on film and then scanning them into digital," he raves about his new camera. "It's fabulously sharp and fast," he says. "It far exceeds what film can realize. It has more tonality, more color range, smoother transitions. It's more sensitive in dark scenes and more responsive to different color temperatures. It has 16 bits of resolution and creates files of 63 megabytes. That's huge."

The challenge to Foveon is that Gorman's new camera is a single-lens reflex called the 1Ds based on CMOS imagers and mosaic filters. It is made entirely by Canon Corporation in Japan.

With ordinary CMOS performing such feats in a professional camera, do the CCD champions skulk away into the night? Hardly. Early in 2004, Sony Corporation, the consumer electronics paragon and champion of CCDs, would emerge with its DSC-F828 Cybershot based on a new four-color filter CCD, adding emerald to the usual red, green, and blue, to reduce color errors by 50 percent and enhance reproduction of treacherous borderline blue-green and red colors where Foveon's technology excels. With 8 megapixels, a Karl Zeiss optical zoom lens, and the capability of doing either high-resolution stills or DVD-quality movies, the new Sony offers a featuristic photocopia. It provides a hologrammatic laser focus for low light, "Night-Framing" for accurately composed photos when using flash, and "NightShot" mode for black-and-white picture taking in total darkness without flash, using infrared illumination, all for an announced price of $1,200, sure to sink soon far below $1,000.

Canon is a dominant force in cameras, Sony is dominant in consumer electronics and CCDs, and they are both pushing their technologies ahead at a tremendous pace. With volumes millions of times greater than Foveon's, Canon and Sony careen down the learning curve, harvesting gains of scale and scope, making their leading-edge imagers and the cameras based on them ever better and cheaper. Carver Mead and the warriors at Foveon faced the complex business challenge of attacking an incumbent industrial establishment. How could they do it?

In every new era, companies prevail by grasping the significance of a new regime of abundances and scarcities. Foveon would have to exploit an amazing new abundance in photographic technology.

Advancing through an interplay between what is available in volume and what is not, entrepreneurs exploit the abundant resources to relieve the scarcities. They use oil to save human muscle, the interior maws and middens of fossils in Earth's center to preserve the scarce arable spaces on the surface. They use silicon to economize on humans unwilling to tote up detail, or abundant bandwidth to obviate scarce local data storage (or storage to compensate for choked connectivity).

If men and nations ignore the abundance, and obsess on the scarcity, they plunge their companies and economies into an abyss of ever-narrowing horizons and possibilities. Men and nations who glimpse the glow of abundance beyond the deserts and culs of scarcity can lead the world toward a promised land.

Abundances end in infinity, with a price of zero. Scarcities end in zero, with a price of infinity.

Power, for example, has become an abundance with a price of a few cents per kilowatt hour for electricity. Wireless power— from batteries—has become a scarcity with a price of a few thousand dollars per kilowatt hour.

Bandwidth has become an abundance, with a price per gigabit per second almost free on worldwide webs of glass and light.

Connectivity has become scarce, with a price of $600 per megabit per second per month down a T-1 line.

Storage has become abundant, with a cost of around 50 cents per gigabyte on new disk drives.

Wireless storage for cameras has become scarce, at a cost of scores of dollars for a gigabyte on a flash card.

Both entrepreneurs and economists live in a world of scarcity. Only entrepreneurs see the abundance beyond.

FOVEON POSSESSED THE secrets of a new canonical abundance: high-resolution low-power imager pixels. In theory, it could combine this abundance with complementary abundances of bandwidth, storage, and wireless connectivity to create a new global paradigm of ubiquitous cheap imaging. But Foveon's abundance was purely theoretical. It could be realized only if Foveon could find markets for a huge volume of its chips.

TAPPING ITS POTENTIAL, Foveon could attack from above, using the X3's high resolution and accuracy to invade the markets for professional single-lens-reflex cameras. That is the strategy being pursued by Sigma. Since Sigma is a leading high-volume producer of lenses, the strategy may work for them. But the relatively small high-end market would leave most of the new abundance untapped by Foveon, while the producers of CCDs and cheap black-and-white imagers took the volume trade. With volumes thousands of times larger than Foveon's, their costs and even their performance might eventually become better despite their relatively cumbrous designs.

After all, the Canon 1Ds celebrated by Gorman was based on an advanced 11-megapixel CMOS imager and mosaic filters.

Foveon's Rich Turner acknowledges that the entire system is beautifully designed. For a high-end camera, the actual imager is a relatively small portion of the price. Canon could dominate this market without ever confronting the technical superiority of the X3.

Perhaps then Foveon could attack from below, using its one-chip cheapness and dual function, still and motion versatility, to enter the mass markets for throwaway cameras, cell-phone imagers, and camcorders. That means changing a company full of photography connoisseurs into a pure low-end imager house—albeit with the world's highest-resolution imagers. That may not be easy to accept. Otherwise Foveon could perhaps attack from the side, pioneering new markets for high-resolution surveillance applications. Or should they risk diffusion of focus by chasing all these markets at once?

As Foveon emerged slowly from stealth and began to market its product in 2003, these strategic issues remained unsettled.

FOR MANY YEARS, the leading competitor for any microchip camera company, digital or analog, was film. But Gorman believes that this era is essentially over for still images. Only in theatrical films in all their forms, from 70mm IMAX to Cinerama, does film continue to hold on against the persistent incursions of digital, and that too may soon change.

At the high end, Foveon's key competition will come not from film or even from Canon and the other Japanese producers, but from Moore's Law itself, as it steadily improves the performance and lowers the price of every digital camera based on silicon regardless of whether it uses Foveon technology or imitates it. Foveon then will face the grim challenge of Drucker's Law: A new system cannot prevail unless it is at least ten times as good as the incumbent system.

Repeating the military defender's edge in an entrenched position, Drucker's Law reflects the momentum, scope, and scale of incumbency. It feeds on the cumulative investment and tacit learning of both consumers and suppliers. If you have learned the intricacies of Microsoft Windows, you are not ready to learn a new operating system that is merely five times faster for many applications. Similarly in cameras, if you have mastered the intuitive lore of manipulating lenses, filters, and f-stops to shape and enhance your picture, you will not welcome a new system, no matter how superior in resolution and simplicity, that relegates many of these functions to post processing in software. Counterintuitive to most people, Drucker's Law explains the inventor's angst (and lawyers' glee) suffusing every conference on patents, as the creators of things "at least two times better, five times better, eight times better" than the prevailing "junk" concoct conspiracy theories of incumbent crime and malice to explain the facts of life.

Subverting the military analogy of Drucker's Law, however, is the counterexample of guerrilla terrorism. Under some circumstances, the attacker has the advantage. He can select one vulnerable point to assault, while the defender has the impossible challenge of preparing for all eventualities. The incumbent does not know what to expect or where, and may underestimate the power of surprise.

"DO YOU THINK me a dog that you contest me with sticks and stones?" roared Goliath, the Philistine giant of biblical times, expressing the contempt usual among established elites toward a disruptive challenge. Confronting rivals from below who fail to observe the rules of "the road ahead," as Bill Gates entitled his first book, powerful incumbents belittle the tools and talents of their upstart rivals. David's slingshot was what Clayton Christensen, the author of *The Innovator's Dilemma* and now *The Innovator's Solution*, calls a "disruptive technology." Defying Drucker's mandate of tenfold superiority, this is a slingshot contraption that could even be tenfold *inferior* by all the prevailing standards and still blow away a regnant Goliath.

Disruptive technology is a treacherous concept, easy to grasp too quickly. Akin to David's disruptive sticks and stones in its surprising effect on a seemingly fixed status quo was the motor car. Hugely inefficient at converting oats to energy, inept at hiking the available trails, prone to constant breakdowns, and supplying no fertilizer for the garden, early automobiles practically required their users to become mechanics. What kind of product was that? Perhaps it was a disrupter. With their obvious advantages in speed and comfort, though, cars seem too clearly superior to equestrian technology to be a clear case in point. Some upstart technologies are so vastly better than the incumbent that they blow it away by raw superiority rather than by disruptive stealth. Perhaps Foveon fits this model, but judging from Gorman's enthusiasm for his Canon, an overwhelming frontal attack will not work for Foveon.

A MORE FAMILIAR and pure disrupter was the personal computer. Based on Faggin's microprocessors and their descendents, early PCs could not execute the graphics, computer-aided engineering, real-time transactions, fast Fourier transforms, and database access that comprised prime functions of established computers. And to use one, you had to become some kind of computer technician. Yet early PCs found a market among hackers, and then infiltrated large companies one by one for use in running spreadsheets. Within ten years between 1977 and 1987, they moved from under 1 percent to over 99 percent of the market for computer power. That's disruption.

DISRUPTION BECOMES POSSIBLE in the face of a new technological paradigm. When a new paradigm arises, advances in the old paradigm—faster horses, bigger mainframes, more accurate and versatile cameras—may offer technology overshoot. The market wants a flyswatter, but industry keeps improving the blunderbuss. Every advance pushes the incumbents deeper into a zone of disruption, what Christensen calls a "failure framework," using gunpowder in ever-more sophisticated ways to kill flies.

In the context of the radical new paradigm of portable instant cellphone cameras or teleputers that can do both still and motion images, advances in conventional digital imagers may bring scores of impressive companies into jeopardy. Heading for the zone of disruption today at a rapid pace may be such companies as Canon and Kodak.

Christensen explains for the first time how disrupters can win even against giants. He shows how inferior tools can prevail against what he calls "sustaining technologies," such as ever-faster mainframes and minicomputers or ever-faster and more cornucopian mosaic digital cameras. Analyzing a wide range of industries, from disk drives to steel mills, from excavators to pharmaceuticals, from motorbikes to electric cars, he brings rare new light to the predicament of the dominant firms in a market. No matter how superior your technology, you may well be attacked from below by vendors of cheap convenient devices that your own customers disdain.

The alleged success of inferior technologies has become a misleading cliché. Unleashing aggressive class-action suits, antitrust lawyers promise to save our economy from a blight of "market failure" and bad product "lock-in." Cited as cases in point are such defective items as QWERTY keyboards, VHS videocasettes, and IBM-Microsoft standard PCs that supposedly won over better designs because of a sly bent of free economies to foster monopolies. In fact, each of the allegedly inferior products was superior in the relevant features, such as ability to record an entire movie (VHS) or 16-bit operation (IBM). Even the QWERTY keyboard turned out to be essentially equal in performance. None of the competitors—Betamax tapes, Apple IIs, and Dvorak keyboards—could begin to meet Drucker's requirement of tenfold superiority.

Christensen's theory has nothing to do with such fables of "market failure." Instead, he cogently explains how markets tend to foster not monopolies but their overthrow.

In part, the inferiority of disrupters is an optical illusion, reflecting the vantage point of the establishment. The new products are inferior only by the prevailing metrics. By other measures they may be hugely or even infinitely superior, since the established tools may not be able to function at all in the new market. For example, no matter how many gigabytes a 5.25-inch disk drive may hold or how superior is its seek-and-rotate time or how much faster its data throughput rate, it could not supply storage for a laptop computer, let alone a camera, with room only for 3.5-inch or smaller disks. In that market, the superiority of the larger disks became suddenly irrelevant. The smaller, slower "inferior" disks were competing not against another technology but against the alternative of doing without. As Christensen says, "Competing not against existing competitors with existing customers but against *nonconsumption*"—against teleputers, cameras, and cell phones with no internal hard drives at all.

Christensen shows that in the history of technology this pattern recurs over and over again. The inexorable dynamics of innovation render dominant companies of one industry paradigm feckless in another.

Since most digital cameras and camcorders currently receive their images through a silicon array of CCD photodetectors, CCDs are now a fast-growing, Japanese-dominated business of some $5 billion, and the pride of wafer fabs from Sony to Sharp. Sony still cherishes high hopes for its future. Shigeyuki Ochi, Sony's venerable semiconductor chief, predicts the ubiquitous use of CCDs for video teleconferencing. Hiroshi Inoue of Sharp agrees: "As we move into the multimedia era, CCDs will be used to capture all sorts of images and send them down phone lines, and all personal computers will have CCDs built into them. . . . Wherever there's a need for something to play the role of the human eye, if it's electronic, it'll be the CCD."

Carver Mead thus did not cause dancing in the clean rooms and design centers of Japan when he visited Tokyo early in the new century to bring the good news that CCDs could be replaced by Foveon's X3 device. Japanese engineers would listen very politely to his case. Then amid various permutations of smiles and bows, they would respond in the same essential way: "When you make your chip behave like a charge-coupled device, so it uses the same power as a CCD and plugs into the same sockets as a CCD and emits the same kinds of signals as a CCD, and exhibits the same noise level as a CCD—and you make it significantly cheaper—then you come back and we will talk to you."

The source of the stubborn opposition is no conspiracy of threatened incumbents or blindness to opportunity. Drucker's mandate of the tenfold advantage applies. Facing Sony and the other Japanese Goliaths, with all their sales momentum, learning-curve progress, knowledge base, cumulative investment, and customer familiarity, Foveon has "no chance" to prevail, declares Christensen, unless it adopts a disruptive strategy. If Foveon goes up head-to-head with the incumbents, "it will lose," he says. In his entire Harvard database of technological innovations, he has catalogued no case of an outsider displacing an incumbent in what he calls a "sustaining" technology—its existing core business.

"Foveon cannot make cameras," he asserts. To win, Foveon must pioneer new markets. It must compete not for existing camera customers but for entirely new customers and applications. Foveon can meet both these requirements. But it has not done it yet.

Returning from Japan without any significant new orders for the X3 beyond Sigma's high-end camera, Mead said: "This is not a problem, it is an opportunity. We are going to make cameras."

NEARLY ALL THE world's executives have learned the apparent lesson of IBM's decision to adopt Intel microprocessors and Microsoft operating systems for the IBM personal computer. Therefore, companies such as Nikon, Kodak, Sony, and Canon will mightily resist pasting "Foveon Inside" on the fronts of their cameras. According to Christensen, Mead will fail if he tries to capture these existing camera markets. Yet following his many trips to Japan to find customers for the X3, Mead believes that in order to demonstrate the superiority of his chips, he will have to make cameras.

The solution to his problem is now emerging. Early in 2003, the Japanese camera journals became the first to recognize the full significance of the Foveon breakthrough. Three leading Japanese photography magazines put on their covers—either alone or with one rival—the image of a new camera, the Sigma SD9, made by a lens company that had never before manufactured a digital camera. Like Intel's logo on a personal computer, the camera bore the distinctive X3 symbol of Foveon. The lead-

ing Japanese digital camera publication—*Digital Photo*—
devoted no fewer than twenty-eight pages to a detailed comparison of the Sigma SD9 with Canon's EOS-1Ds single-lens-reflex
camera. The journal concluded that although the Canon possessed certain advantages in ease of use, the resolution and
verisimilitude of the Sigma were essentially equal or superior in
every category. Operating near the peak of their resolution, the
Canon CMOS imagers suffer from the distortions inevitable
with some five filters in front of every pixel. Included is even a
$1,000 "blur" filter to smear away color artifacts that result from
the inability of the chip to define colors near borders between
two different hues. Without any way for a digital signal processor to re-create information that has been thrown away, the only
alternative is to blur the colors together.

Although camera technology connoisseurs such as Merrill
and Mead can detect these flaws, Canon's digital processing is
so brilliantly performed that it is invisible even to professional
photographers.

With all the other features honed to perfection, this Canon
camera is the very same machine that so captivated Greg Gorman. It is the device that prompted him to assert the obsoles-
cence of his cherished film. Even Foveon's own experts agree
that the Canon 1Ds is a superb camera, about as good as digital
photography can get. But it costs some five times as much as the
Sigma camera using the Foveon X3.

Inside the pages of *Digital Photography* was a full portfolio of
photographs from the two cameras. To the lay person, there
seemed to be no discernible difference in quality. The Sigma

camera proved that the Foveon technology was sufficiently pow-erful and effective in its initial form to be introduced near the top of the market. But the expensive Canon camera used a com-plex multifiltered imaging system, while the Sigma camera embodied all its crucial image reception and processing in just one chip. That chip might ultimately be manufactured in vol-ume for as little as a dollar.

As Merrill explains, "The fundamental advantage of the verti-cal color filter technology is its two-and-a-half-to-three-times greater efficiency in the use of any particular silicon area or lens quality. With a lens of given quality that can resolve a spot of given size, Foveon can measure three times more information than can a CCD with a plastic color filter." Silicon area is a rough index of unit cost, so three times the efficiency in the use of silicon area means one-third the chip cost. Lens quality com-pounds this advantage, since for any particular level of image quality, Foveon can use a lens with one-third the focal area (which means far less than one-third the cost).

As Foveon's volumes increase, its imager is moving into cheaper applications. Because of its supremely low power, it can be incorporated in every cell phone handset, imparting a joint ability to render both still and motion images. With a potential market of billions, cell phones are now the most common digital machines and represent the largest market for imagers. From cell phones, Foveon can move to every computer screen for video teleconferencing, which is the next major broadband Internet application. Multiple Foveon chips can be deployed for surveillance in every convenience store and gas station and can guard every automatic teller machine. Foveon imagers can survey every security point in every airport.

Fulfilling the Christensen mandate, the Foveon device can eventually become ubiquitous without ever challenging any incumbent camera company for its current customers. It is then—not before—that the Foveon chip might move massively into the mainstream camera market.

This is the disruptive path of Foveon's triumph. It is the "innovator's solution" that Christensen is proposing in his new book. Foveon will compete not chiefly against existing products but against nonconsumption of imagers. By making the imaging function cheap and robust, Foveon can open huge new markets for its innovation.

Foveon's ultimate achievement will depend on the continued onrush of digital electronics. Each Foveon picture ultimately translates into a digital file of up to 40 megabytes (millions of characters; this book is less than one megabyte). In order for Foveon pictures to take over the world of photography and film, these dense images will require broadband communications and trillions of bytes of storage in a combination that I have dubbed "storewidth." Mead's analog technologies will change the world, but the world will also have to change to accommodate these new capabilities.

Intel and Microsoft are among the leaders in moving Foveon toward mainstream applications. Intel has staked much of its future on the success of wireless broadband communications. To transmit Foveon's streams of images from surveillance devices or cell phones will entail ever more wireless bandwidth.

Now spreading through "hot spots" across the country from Bryant Park in Manhattan to Dallas–Fort Worth Airport, from the top of the Mark to Starbuckses everywhere, WiFi in both the 2.4-gigahertz and 5-gigahertz bands can play a key role in public places and offices. However, in accord with Merrill's rule—no camera is satisfactory unless you want to take it mountain climbing—photography is not restricted to "hot spots." More relevant to Foveon will be Qualcomm's CDMA 2000 EV-DO technology that can endow broadband imager capabilities everywhere that cell phone systems are deployed.

Preparing for the Foveon revolution in software is Microsoft. When Bill Gates launched his XP-network-based operating system at a trade show, this king of the digital age did not begin by entering a password or clicking icons in a pop-up window. Instead he put his finger firmly on a glowing biometric touch pad that recognized Gates, loaded his personal settings, and gave him access to his personal files and digital kingdom. The company that supplied this open sesame is called Digital Persona. But its innovation in pattern matching is analog and its technical leader, Vance Bjorn, a former Mead student, represents another fruit of Carver's campaign to transform the world of analog interfaces to the digital world.

Microsoft has also developed a new standard for representing photographs on the net. The GIFs and JPEGs of the current World Wide Web are grossly inadequate to capture the vividness and verisimilitude of Foveon pictures. As new standards are perfected, the world of the Net will be able to render yet another image of a cat—a cougar, in the act of leaping off the screen toward you. Mead's revolutionary camera will make your computer brim with the intense dynamic colors of a new era. Like the apparent glass on the top of the pile of carpets, your screen will disappear into a luminous new world of art and color.

Still, the most poignant feline symbol of the amazing advances achieved by the company is the picture on the wall outside Mead's corner office at Foveon. It is a three-foot-high image of the face of a cat. It is based on the same essential silicon technology used twelve years before in the *Scientific American* cover heralding the first working retina chips made by Mead and Mahowald. But rather than the blurry monochromatic sketch offered on that old magazine cover, the new image offers a full-color vividness and verisimilitude rarely excelled in photography of any kind. Some six square feet, the image resolves every hair, whisker, glint, and gleam of the feline fur and renders the eyes of the cat with a lifelike glow that gives the viewer the distinct and disturbing feeling that a formidable animal is watching him. Yet the picture is of a kitten.

To fulfill the promise of kitten or cougar, however, Foveon would have to find new leadership that could take the company down market into the realms of disruption where in its path would be live cougars galore.

23

Holy Kammoli!

O n his daily dawn walk in the Arastradero Preserve, intently chatting in Italian with Alvia, his wife of thirty-six years, Federico Faggin met a cougar in his path. Early in the twenty-first century, cougars, terrorists, class-action lawyers, and other feral creatures all "had their rights" and had begun to gain an edge on humans in Silicon Valley. Faggin had seen several big cats around his home in the Los Altos Hills. Admiring the sleek feline, Federico and Alvia waited for it to cross over into the sepia grasses and twisted trees on the uphill side of the road. Then they made their way briskly down the mountain.

Entering his sixties, Faggin was no longer inclined to confront large predators, whether sepia or silicon. Graying at the temples, with a jaunty gait, dimply smile, and a modest paunch, he was slowly retiring into the Silicon Valley role of "gentleman investor." "After all," so he says with a gay chortle, "in the Los Altos Hills, I could hardly be a gentleman farmer."

By dint of the insistence of Alvia, who gently but persistently corrected any journalists or historians who erred in their chronicles of her legendary husband, the world now increasingly recognized Faggin as the true father of the microprocessor and the silicon-gate process that made it possible. As a biological father, proud of their artist daughter, Marzia, and their two sons, he had also done well. Eric, twenty-three, was a graduate in physics and philosophy at Santa Clara, making a leisurely survey of the universe, and the other son, Marc, twenty-four, had done a double major in math and chemistry and then plunged deep in pursuit of a doctorate at Cornell, in nanotechnology. "I'll leave that to him," Faggin said with a smile.

In the Los Altos Hills, he found himself surrounded on all sides by local venturers and investors devastated first by the technology crash and then by the new century's long doldrums in initial public offerings. But Faggin had mostly emerged unscathed. After scoring handsomely in Synaptics, which had the first and only major Silicon Valley IPO of 2002, he had invested some $400,000 in Foveon with New Enterprise Associates (NEA), the eminent venture capitalists led by Richard Kramlich. He looked forward to the success of this promising technology in the midst of a booming market for imagers. Later he joined the board of Blue Arc, the preeminent success in hardware for storage networking, a British company initially guided and financed by Italian friend Walter Allesandrini and run by another Italian friend Gianlucca Rattazzi. Faggin also became a director of the Allesandrini telecom equipment start-up, Avanex, which soared during the optics boom, collapsed in 2000, and then morphed into a successful scavenger among the ruins, picking up optical divisions from Alcatel and Corning.

Becoming a laureled lion in the Valley, Faggin even received a call from Jim Thornburn of Zilog, the company begun by Faggin and Masatoshi Shima when they defected from Intel (Shima later returned to Intel to head its Japanese research facility). Faggin had broken entirely with Zilog in 1981 and, until the mid-1990s, the company had subsisted on sales of billions of Z-8s and Z-80s, microprocessors embedded in automobiles, toys, kitchen white goods, and microwave ovens. Then Texas-Pacific Corporation decided to cash in on the telecom boom by taking the company private and relaunching it into the hot new market for network processors—microprocessors used to run networks.

Milking cash from the Z-80 to support entry into the communications chip business where it had no special competence, Zilog built a $700 million wafer fab and nearly went bankrupt. Thorburn asked Faggin for guidance in returning the company to its roots as an embedded microprocessor firm based on the Z-8. Engaging in a rare Silicon Valley success in the enterprise of nostalgia, Faggin enjoyed helping in the revival of his design from some thirty-five years before.

In the late summer of 2003, the Faggins left for a vacation in China. Both looked forward to more exciting travel as the years passed.

FOVEON, MEANWHILE, WAS in the throes of a series of turbulent board meetings. Under a search team composed of Dick

Kramlich and Forrest Baskett of New Enterprise Associates (NEA), Dick Sanquini, formerly of National Semiconductor, and the absent Faggin, the board was attempting to find a new CEO who could take the company across the chasm from a few high-end cameras to the promised land of billions of cell phones. Under prompting from NEA, the Foveon board hired Lonergan Richards, a Silicon Valley headhunter, to conduct a nationwide search. Faggin would presumably be covering China.

Previously chosen by Faggin as his chief financial officer at Synaptics, interim Foveon CEO Jim Lau was a competent corporate leader. An engaging man, with a friendly smile, everyone liked him. As the organizer of Synaptics's intricate web of Asian manufacturers, Lau had been crucial to the success of Faggin's previous company. Lau would continue to serve Foveon as a CFO who also possessed a sharp understanding of the manufacturing mazes of Asia. But in marketing he was cautious. He didn't like to offend competitors by making grand claims of superiority for Foveon's imager. Under Lau, Foveon did not assert that its pixels were worth between two and three CCD pixels. That would be aggressive. Talking to journalists, Lau was a master of the "no comment." He was no cougar. And now his company was being passed by rivals with inferior products. As the board members met, they became increasingly alarmed at the condition of the company that Lau had been leading.

Full of photographers indignant about the artifacts and distortions inherent in most digital cameras, Foveon had targeted the top of the camera market, where Carver Mead three years earlier at Photokina 2000 had uncovered one avid customer,

Sigma. But in the subsequent years under Lau's leadership, no further buyers of the Foveon chip had emerged. Nor were there many customers for Sigma's much-honored but still-exotic camera, which Sigma treated chiefly as a loss leader, a way to sell Sigma's estimable line of lenses. On the board of directors, Brian Halla of National Semiconductor brought everyone down to earth by comparing Foveon's search for customers to "a fellow with a metal detector combing the beach."

.

FOVEON'S CHIEF HOPE for a breakthrough at the bottom of the market was Sanyo, the major independent Japanese manufacturer of mass-market digital cameras, including Nikon's popular Coolpix model. Ask anyone at Foveon about customers beyond Sigma and those in the know talking to those with a right to know would cite Sanyo, sure to sign any day now. Foveon's marketing department under Allen Rush had been negotiating with Sanyo for nearly two years. All the reports were "highly promising, deep interest, excited by the technology," but somehow no deal was closed. "You know how those big Japanese companies are. Takes them forever," Mead told me.

Now in the fall of 2003, with cell phone imagers from other companies selling in the millions, the board mandated Lau to close a deal. Lau went to Sanyo in September 2003 and secured a meeting in Tokyo with the top executives in the company. The top Sanyo executives turned out to care little about Foveon. Lau reported to the board that while the lower-level engineers were enthusiastic about the Foveon sensors X3 and X19, the senior executives were open chiefly to using them as a foil to force down prices from rival vendors of CCDs and CMOS imagers that fit snugly in CCD slots.

When Faggin returned from China in September, he began to hear distressing reports on Foveon. On his walks in the mountains with Alvia, he expressed increasing frustration at the slow development of any visible results. "What is wrong with this picture?" he asked. He was beginning to doubt what he had been told about the superiority of the technology. Sure it was better to capture all the light at every pixel, but the CCD was not standing still. It reminded him of the experience at Intel when the company perfected its dynamic random access memory (DRAM). Bob Noyce and Gordon Moore projected that the DRAM would displace the regnant magnetic-core memories in two or three years. But challenged by the DRAM, core memory engineers improved the cost effectiveness of cores tenfold over the next five years. The DRAM's triumph was delayed by half a decade. Now Faggin at board meetings heard Mead (himself a CCD inventor) and Merrill declare that CCD makers would not be able to reduce their pixel size below 5 microns square (25 square microns). Challenged by CMOS imagers, including Foveon's X3, however, CCD engineers at Sony and Canon soon managed to reduce their pixel size to 4 microns square. CCD pixels were soon not only smaller than Foveon scientists believed possible but smaller than Foveon itself could then make at its National Semiconductor fab. Dick Lyon insisted that the smaller pixels yielded worse images. Less light was collected per pixel. More errors. But the fact remained that the CCD was on track to put three pixels, together with admittedly tricky plastic color filters, in a space that Foveon could put one three-transistor vertical pixel. So what was this huge advantage? A matter of design and taste. Yes, the Foveon pixel would be far more elegant, use less power, and so on. But Foveon still would have a serious problem persuading anyone to throw out their old CCD technology in favor of a new device that did not even yield smaller pixels and thus did not even allow Foveon to claim leadership in the heralded "can-you-top-this" megapixel sweepstakes.

But then, under Lau and Allen Rush, Foveon was not even claiming more pixels, except by the backhand "times 3" after the 3.6 megapixel number (even though the "times 3" was always elided in press reports). Foveon's marketers had allowed themselves to be intimidated by the Japanese from even asserting that with three colors at every spot a Foveon pixel was worth 3 one-color pixels on a CCD or ordinary CMOS imager. Foveon's 3.6 megapixels were actually 11 megapixels. "Better be conservative," said the Foveon marketers. "Better be wrong, and lose," said Faggin.

Faggin argued that the board could not find a promising CEO until it determined what the problem was. He offered to investigate. Then as he began his inquiry, he realized that he could not succeed in diagnosing the problem unless he had full power to probe anywhere in the company. He suggested that he replace Lau as interim CEO.

BY THE NEXT board meeting in September, Faggin was ready to take over. Before leaving on his search for powerline artifacts in the Appalachians, Mead had one final meeting with Faggin.

"Faggin chose to have one of his hissy fits," Carver recalls. "According to him, no one had done anything right since the founding of the company. Before he took over, he wanted to show to everyone that the situation was nearly impossible—that no one else knew what they were doing—that only he could save the day. He built himself up. But in the process he was building up the pressure, the intensity, the competitiveness he needed to do the job. Much of what he said was exaggerated. We all knew that Sigma was not the final solution. We all knew we had to enter the cell-phone market. But that said, there was no doubt that he had a much better view of the competitive situation than any of us had."

Faggin's investigation had persuaded him that Mead was a passive chairman who had allowed the company to go off track. "Mead was infatuated with the technology. He knew all the advantages, in principle. He was in love with the theory. When you are infatuated, you cannot see the flaws. . . ."

Faggin concluded that in principle the Foveon process was indeed superior to charge-coupled devices and CMOS digital imagers. But in its existing form it was not superior in practice. And in the imager business, as opposed to the image business, the market for principles remained small.

FROM TIME TO time over the years, Carver Mead and Faggin had clashed. Carver was always listening to the technology, while Faggin was listening to the market. Mead normally angled to open up technological possibilities, while Faggin sought to anneal them into a sword. But just as Faggin had previously deferred to Mead in shaping the technology, at this point Mead readily deferred to Faggin in running the company, believing that it now needs Faggin's marketeering insight and strategic resourcefulness more than it needs his own technology insight. And Faggin is no slouch on technology either.

Reflecting on experience with twenty companies, Mead mused on the Foveon saga: "It's what happens when you start a company. The unlimited potential of your new technology. It's a huge high just thinking about it. But once it is manifest, once it becomes a product, it's not a myriad of anything—it's one thing. . . . It's happened with every company I've worked with— they get to the point where they're successful, they're on track, and there's less and less that someone like me can contribute. You actually become a distraction—they're trying to focus and you're wandering around thinking about all these interesting new questions. That's when it's time to leave."

Concluding that Faggin was the right man to lead the company, Mead observed: "He doesn't take a lot of input. I am always seeking win-win situations, but Federico is a fighter. He loves a good fight. And today Foveon is in the midst of a fight. All the Japanese want to knock it off. None wants to give in. And no one can fight more resourcefully than Federico.

"I am having the time of my life *not* having to do this," says Mead. "Foveon could not be in better hands."

Faggin was focusing fiercely. "A small company has a limited runway," he commented. "If you don't gain lift before the runway is over, you see the fence coming ahead . . . and it's Holy Kammoli!"

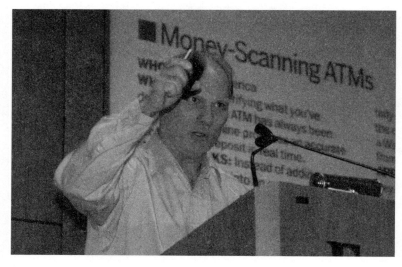

Dick Merrill tells the Telecosm conference about the myriad new appli-cations for cheap, high-resolution imagers. Glenn Davis

24

Foveon RAW in Vegas

I t couldn't happen to a guru more digitally Delphic than John Dvorak, beetle-browed futurist, nerd supreme, *PC* magazine doppelguru, cynical seer through the industry's swell and jiggle to the raw silicone below, virtuoso italicizer, brazen imbolder, crazy new talent at the Consumer Electronics Show, serial keynoter at the Photography Marketing Association, maturing as a vamp in Vegas as familiar as Cirque de Soleil or Penn and Teller and proud owner of a free Sigma 10 camera.

From the record-breaking January 2004 Consumer Electronics Show a month earlier, full of HDTV specs and scams, so goes the story at Foveon corporation, Dvorak went on to the wedding of a friend. When the photographer failed to show, Big John saw his chance. He would take the wedding pictures. He would become: John Dvorak, official photographer, which is a lot easier I can tell you than expectorating two pithy columns, full of **bravado** in bold, and *i-pinions* in italics, every two weeks for *PC* magazine.

Under a canopy on a sunny day, the wedding unfolded blithely with a dark foreground and bright background for all the images. If there had been a professional photographer, he would have been gnashing his apertures and filters. But Big John didn't notice. He just clicked away relentlessly. Just like columns. Write enough of them, with enough pungent wild-eyed predictions, and if you are Dvorak many will prove to be amazingly on target and your column will be a gas to read. More is more. More is better. Take enough photo shots and some of them will be great, right? And with this super new digital camera bearing the Foveon X3 imager that collects all the light and all the colors at every pixel, he couldn't go wrong. His host sure was lucky to have all that extra luminance and chrominance of a beautiful day and lucky to have Big John to memorialize the event for the ages.

Arriving home, Dvorak booted up the Sigma Photo Pro software, linked the camera to his computer with a universal serial bus (USB), rendered his harvest in JPEGs (the familiar compression standard of the Joint Photographic Experts Group that is ubiquitous on the Web), and prepared to bask in the magnificence of his work. But what is this garbage on his screen? Dvorak was shocked. Every picture he took was under the dark canopy with the bright background and every picture was dungeon dark with a dazzling halo. In botching the scene in the same way each and every time, the Sigma was entirely robust and reliable.

With JPEG images—a global compression algorithm—there was no way to fix it. Change the settings and you just get new permutations of bad pictures. You darken it enough to mitigate the blinding brightness outside, and the bride's face disappears under the shadowy canopy. Brighten up the face, and the outside scene "whites out" along with the wedding dress. Ready to write the experience off, perhaps with a column dissing Sigma, he made a plaintive call back to Eric Zarakov at Foveon.

No problem, says Eric. This is the digital era, John, just as you said last year giving your friendly keynote advice to all the artsy-crafty analog photographers, moldy fig film retailers, and proprietors of cramped little photography shops that they might as well all just skulk away and use their stores to rent DVDs, because it was time to sing a Hallelujah chorus of digital *über alles*. And you were right. Once again a prophet in your own time. But for the full-scale Foveon effect, you have to use the correct digital format. For redeeming botched exposures, you can't use JPEG. You have to do it Vegas style, in the RAW. The pure undressed, uncompressed output from the light sensors on the camera in digital form. All the bits and bytes from the scene arrayed in an image frame. It will look awful, but don't panic, it is totally accurate; all the information is there.

With just one simple shift of the Hubel FillLite slider bar in your Sigma Pro software, moving it to a level of perfect balance of light and shadow—even hours, days, or years after exposure— you can cook up the RAW data and serve it *au point*. The darkness will be made light and the brightness will be made mute, and the luminance lines will lie down with the chrominance lambdas and all will be well. And so it was.

By early February, when he rekeynoted the Photography Marketing Association bash, also in Las Vegas, Dvorak was an ecstatic member of the Foveon cult. He had experienced the benefits of a real accurate window (RAW) at every pixel coupled with FillLite, a simple ingenious software algorithm contrived by a hiree of Dick Lyon named Paul Hubel. FillLite is not exactly unique. Given accurate RAW files, Photoshop and other software conversion programs can do it with an array of some six different adjustments. But Hubel had made it simple and elegant and fun to use. Just slide the bar, in either the positive or negative direction, into the sun or into the shade, until the picture suits your dream. Professionals may cavil, but afterwards in *PC* magazine, Dvorak was right to be bold and italicized.

On the crest of the digital revolution, the 2004 PMA show was the organization's eightieth and the biggest ever, with 17,000 exhibits, mostly digital cameras and accessories, sprawling over fifteen acres, or a million square feet of show floor on two levels of the South End of the Vegas Convention Center off Paradise Avenue (occupying the North End near the Hilton were the spruce armies of the Gun and Rifle Dealers' show, prompting many comments on the comparative firepower of digital cameras and machine guns).

As Dvorak had long predicted, digital turned out not to be the death of photography but its efflorescence. In 2003, worldwide digital imager sales of nearly 50 million exceeded the experts' consensus of 38 million by over one-third. Commandingly the product of the year, the digital camera in all its manifestations is giving vision to computers and telephones, twenty-four-hour vigilance to ATM machines, taxicabs and convenience stores, and high resolution to cheap, adaptable cameras. And the theme of the PMA convention was RAW. Sashimi, sushi, Canon, Sony, Nikon, Konica, Minolta, and Olympus. But the big news, for those who knew the plot, was Foveon, which sold a nearly imperceptible share of those 50 million imagers but offered the best raw files of all.

Dvorak, Markoff of the *New York Times*, and Chris Anderson, editor of *Wired*, all knew the plot, so they covered the show much as if it were a Foveon product launch. For the *Times*, Markoff's piece, his third on Foveon, appeared on the front page of the business section on Monday of convention week. *USA Today* and the initial issue of the convention tabloid also featured the new Foveon product. To the industry-leading cost performance of the Sigma10 digital single-lens reflex (DSLR), Foveon had added the industry-leading cost performance of a point-and-shoot camera and DVD quality VGA (video graphics array) camcorder for an announced $399.

Still, Foveon in Vegas was chiefly in demonstration mode. The new point-and-shoot camera did not spring from some brilliant new partnership with Kodak or Sanyo or Nikon. It bore the somewhat tarnished name of Polaroid. But it was not made by Polaroid either. Polaroid was emerging from bankruptcy with an array of instant digital kiosk printers, cameras, and Polaroid legacy gear that was finding new life in the digital era. But under the stresses of its financial crisis it had licensed its name for digital cameras to an Italian from Hong Kong named Giovanni Tomaselli, head of a firm called World Wide Licenses Limited. Surely you have heard of WWLL. It is an important design and manufacturing subsidiary of an even better-known company called the Character Group PLC. CG-PLC, as the Foveon folk were quick to stress, is listed on the London Stock Exchange in the Media and Photography Sector, just in case you are so benighted as never to have heard of the Character Group PLC. Marketing the camera in the United States, however, would be Uniden. Don't ask. It is the familiar Japanese vendor of cordless telephones and exclusive U.S. distributor of Polaroid digital cameras, which as you may recall are manufactured by World Wide Licenses Limited of Hong Kong and in one instance employ an X3 imager from Foveon.

In the midst of this magpie's nest of commercial and manufacturing entities lies the pearl of Foveon's intellectual property and conceptual superiority, which Dvorak came to appreciate at the wedding and which to nearly everyone in Foveon's circle seems resplendent and undeniable. The inelegance of the competitors' Bayer filter color routine is evident even in the twisted language it evokes. The result of using filters to focus light of only a single primary color on each pixel sensor, the conventional Bayer pattern is a mosaic of red, green, or blue pixels. A processor is needed to compute the actual colors from the colors of adjacent pixels.

Describing the process of converting a Bayer pattern into a usable RAW file—here Foveon chief scientist Lyon's lips pucker with distaste—are terms such as *demosaic* and *de-Bayer*, *de-jag* and *de-alias*. Accurate from the outset, Foveon's colors do not need to be demosaiced and their edges do not have to be "blur filtered" and "de-jagged," and their patterns do not need

"de-aliasing" so you can see every last curlicue in the swirly
design on Carver Mead's shirt.

TO FOVEON'S PARTISANS, it was obvious that the company
had its rivals surrounded on all sides. You want perfect top-of-
the-line pictures and you get the Sigma 10 for $1,200. You want
high-resolution high-accuracy point-and-shoot, with 4.5
megapixels, 12x zoom, RAW files, and FillLite software, and you
can buy that too in the Polaroid x530. You want a camcorder,
thirty frames a second of full motion VGA video and you can get
it from that same point-and-shoot device.

Dick Lyon could explain to you the intrinsic inferiority of all
the hundreds of other cameras with slightly different features
glittering across the pullulating floor. They may have had smaller
pixels (and more "megapixels"), but each of those pixels held less
electric charge and thus could capture less dynamic range (vari-
ation between its darkest and brightest level) and was more sensitive to noise. Plastic color filters over every pixel were a kludge
compared to using the silicon itself as a filter. The picture
would be worse, as Sony discovered with its new 12-megapixel
camera—and don't even mention the fiasco of the new
14-megapixel Kodak.

Supporting Lyon's claims was Lawrence Matson, one of the
earliest Sigma enthusiasts and a staunch defender of the faith
among the professional photographers on the *DP Review* photography Web site. Flying in from Switzerland to attend the
Vegas unveiling, Matson recounted the original excitement he

felt in encountering Foveon imagers. He cited early Sigma photos (even as seen on the Web!) of eyes reflecting the sky without distortion—of a frog's eye mirroring an expanse of blue sky and clouds, or the eye of a cormorant suffused with a span of heavenly blue. He described a portrait of an old man with a single curl of white hair precisely distinguishable. Perfectly rendered in a Sigma portrait, Matson said, "that hair in a Bayer mosaic would become a blue-and-red rope or a 'barber pole.' "

Because of the accurate borders between colors, Foveon etches sharp edges that give its pictures a three-dimensional property, with images seeming almost holographic. In order to avoid "jaggies," mosaic cameras use "blur filters." "That gives Canon images what their devotees like to call 'buttery smooth' textures," said Mattson. "I call it Nutella. It makes the transitions smooth but it also flattens out the picture."

Just as important for the future of still and motion combo cameras, the Bayer burden also afflicts full-motion images. Because of the difficulty of processing huge raw files thirty times per second, all systems for full-motion capture must cluster adjacent pixels and process them together. But non-Foveon imagers cannot readily cluster neighboring pixels because in a mosaic the adjacent pixels capture different colors. They would combine into chrominance murk. The Bayer-based cameras thus have to perform time-consuming and image-distorting digital acrobatics to join together the pixels of the same color. With Foveon, the combination of neighboring pixels was natural, simple, fast, and accurate.

In theory, all the Foveon claims were true and had been true for several years. The Foveon design, in one form or other, would ultimately dominate photography. Dramatizing the business challenge faced by Foveon, however, were the exhibits all around them on the floor of PMA. As CEO and microprocessor co-inventor Federico Faggin put it, "In principle, Foveon is far better, but in practice it is not." Canon, Sony, Samsung, and the others might have to push their technology harder to get a performance comparable to Foveon's but they had the clout to do it. If Sony's CCD colors were distorted, add yet another Bayer filter with emerald hue to correct them. If existing Canon CMOS imagers produced jaggies, make the pixels so small that the jaggies are invisible to the naked eye.

If people judge imagers by the number of megapixels, build wafer fabs with 12-inch (300-millimeter) wafers holding more than twice as many chips as current 8-inch wafers and inscribe the pixel transistors with geometries of 45 nanometers, about a third the size of most current technologies (130 nanometers). Sony and Samsung were already planning to build such factories. If Foveon cameras are intrinsically cheaper to make, produce Samsungs and Sonys in such volumes that manufacturing scale dwarfs the imager edge.

Meanwhile, make sure that all the other features of your camera are superior and multiply the features year by year. No matter how good the Foveon imager is, what is the chance that WWL Limited and "Polaroid" will eclipse Canon and the rest of the Japanese in overall camera quality? And if the large-volume orders go to the Japanese camera giants, the quality of their imagers, by brute force of scope and scale, will also likely eke ahead.

THAT IS THE message from the semiconductor industry. Volume rules quality. Long experience in the semiconductor trade has confirmed the validity of [Nick] Tredennick's Law: *Go for volume and you get quality. Go for quality and you forgo volume and eventually quality as well.* As the chief designer of the high-quality Motorola "68000" microprocessor, Nick knows whereof he speaks. Chiefly used in relatively low-volume Macintosh computers, it was eventually eclipsed by once-inferior PCs based on Intel 8600 family microprocessors. The x86 line sold in such volumes that they attracted enough investment and learning-curve improvement to become dominant in quality as well.

Now the same process is befalling cameras. This phenomenon dooms Foveon to a "spiral of decline," declares Karl Guttag, an eminent former Texas Instruments inventor/engineer with 123 patents mostly in graphics and imaging. A relentless critic of Foveon on *DP Review*, Guttag believes that Foveon can never gain the momentum to make money.

Yet the power of volume will be the ultimate source of Foveon's coming dominance in imagers. All the talk of pure camera refinements will dwindle into commercial irrelevance in the future, when high-volume imager leadership is set in the market for cell phones. In 2003, the world's largest unit seller of cameras was already not Canon or Sony but cell-phone titan Nokia. In the course of time, the highest-quality imagers for the mass market would come from the cell-phone imager market, already 150 million units in 2004 and set to double again in 2005.

All the greater simplicity and elegance of the Foveon imager can translate into a decisive edge in cell phones. The power consumption of CCDs will ultimately prove to be a showstopper for battery-based devices. Against CCDs, Foveon's RAW efficiency yields a fivefold power advantage. Against low-power CMOS (complementary metal oxide semiconductor) imagers, the Foveon stacked pixels yield at least a twofold resolution and accuracy advantage, and the ability simply to cluster pixels means a decisive advantage in camcorder applications.

So emerge the lineaments of the coming world conflict in photography. Foveon first would face off against the photography establishment of Canon, Sony, Nikon, and Olympus backed up by a second team of Fuji, Konica, Minolta, Pentax, Hewlett-Packard, and Kodak, and then it would have to confront the imperial pretensions of Nokia, Samsung, Kyocera, Casio, and a host of others rushing into the cell-phone space. Nearing midpoint in the first decade of the new century the score remained essentially 100 percent market share for the establishment team, essentially 100 percent for Bayer mosaics.

Fighting alone against this massive array of established rivals, as Clayton Christensen declared four years earlier, Foveon has "zero" chance of success. As Faggin says, "Obviously we are going to need partners." For the necessary reinforcements, he was clearly not going to depend chiefly on National Semiconductor, Sigma, and the Character Group. At the show in Vegas, he was busy seeking partners and finding more every day. Foveon's partners would take the company into the new markets for low-power, high-resolution imagers where the war would be won.

The argument for Foveon is that it is intrinsically simply a better technology in every way. For Foveon, therefore, the chief shadow on the show was the notion that the best technology often does not win. In the *Times*, John Markoff reported speculation that Foveon might become the "Betamax" of the digital image revolution. The difference between Foveon and Betamax, though, is that Foveon is indeed decisively superior: five times superior to CCDs in power efficiency and some 2.5 times superior to CMOS mosaics in efficiency of light capture and far superior in superfast full-motion and stop-motion functions, all adding up to the necessary tenfold edge. Indeed for many low-power, high-resolution applications, there is no alternative. In the case of Foveon, there is no tradeoff in which CCDs or CMOS mosaics offer some virtue that the Foveon technology lacks. The superiority of the Canon, Sony, Nikon lineup is their momentum, brand recognition, manufacturing prowess, and financial and marketing clout. All are powerful assets, but they do not eclipse the superiority of Foveon's intrinsic technology in a new world where the camera disappears into the fabric of every location that needs to be imaged or protected.

WITH FOVEON CHALLENGED and many of my telecosmic champions in doubt or doldrums, I am inclined to be churlish. But following Mead's call to "listen to the technology," I still find myself rising in joy at its reveille, which is sounding with new urgency. Like the railroads that bankrupted a previous generation of visionary entrepreneurs and built the foundations of an industrial nation, fiber-optic webs, storewidth breakthroughs, data centers, and wireless systems installed over the last five years will enable and endow the next generation of entrepreneurial wealth.

Mead sums up: "During the bubble I was in the middle of starting Foveon. It was horrible. It was an absolutely awful experience. You couldn't find space. You couldn't get your vendors to answer the phone call. You couldn't get fab runs. You couldn't hire people. They were all being sucked off into these brain-dead companies that didn't have a business plan, but were pounding on their chests and going public in three months, and you could not start a sensible business. We struggled and struggled and struggled. The hardest thing I ever had to do in my life was to get a company going during the bubble.

"Now," he continues, "there's space available; you can get fab runs; you can get vendors to answer the phone. You can make deals with people; you can sit down and they don't spend their whole time telling you how they're a hundred times smarter than you. It's absolutely amazing. You can actually get work done now, which means what's happening now is that the entrepreneurs, the technologists, are building the next generation of technology that isn't visible yet but upon which will be built the biggest expansion of productivity the world has ever seen." On the edge of the network, new semiconductor and optical innovations will bring radical new technologies to market across the span of microcosm and telecosm.

Synaptics has already taken 70 percent of the touch-pad business and now supplies haptic technology for iPods and other devices. Foveon could ultimately take a similar share of the imager market. National Semiconductor retains 30 percent of Foveon and is manufacturing its revolutionary devices in a leading-edge fab in Portland, Maine. Foveon's new silicon imagers are the single most elegant new commercial invention in electronics I have encountered since first meeting Mead at the Marriott at Newark Airport in New Jersey in 1983. Foveon can dominate the next era of the Web as it becomes a broadband vessel of images and videos superior in resolution and quality to analog films.

Following Synaptics and Foveon will be several other Mead companies. Chaired by Mead and based on technology designed by Mead student Chris Di Orio is Impinj, a radical innovator in self-adaptive semiconductors. Located in Seattle, Impinj has achieved the goal of robust analog floating-gate technology envisaged by Federico Faggin at the launch of Synaptics. Impinj chips can be trimmed or adapted after production by adjusting the charges on the floating gates. One of the first products will be a tiny analog radio frequency tag, usable everywhere from superstores to transport containers. But with the aim of drastically lowering the power usage of cell phones, Impinj is also applying its technology to an array of low-power mixed-signal devices.

A further Mead-inspired venture is Audience, offering a probable breakthrough in speech recognition. Launched by Lloyd Watts, formerly at Synaptics, and based in part on Mead's cochlear researches and on Dick Lyon's cochlear model, Audience shows that the key problem of speech recognizers is not digital pattern matching but analog audio reception. A kindred company, also associated with Mead's cochlear researches, called Sonic Innovations, has created directional hearing aids. Emerging in 1999 in Salt Lake City, it has become the fastest-growing company in the global hearing-aid business.

This jumble of apparently unrelated ventures embodies the singular new vision unleashed by Mead some twenty years ago in his classes at Caltech and brought to diverse fruition by an amazingly ingenious cohort of his students and associates from Misha to Lyon. There have been many setbacks on the long trail toward the Foveon revolution, and there will be further setbacks ahead. But these and hundreds of other comparable innovations signal the first hot flare of revival from the devastation of the millennial crash in technology.

Epilogue
Camera's End

In moments of weakness and enthusiasm, Mead, Faggin, Merrill, and Lyon at Foveon speak of transforming the camera business. Perhaps, *en passant*, they may achieve this goal. But as a target, it will lead them astray. A more plausible and practical goal is to dismantle the camera altogether and diffuse it throughout the world.

Both in the etymology of the word and in the history of the device, a "camera" is a curved room, a vaulted chamber, an arched vestibule, a cavernous black box. *In camera* the judge meets privately with Perry Mason, to upbraid him for rhetorical excesses. In a *camera obscura*—an original dark room—pictures shone on a wall from a lensed hole that passed light in from outside. Often made in the form of a circular building, the *camera obscura* enclosed a group of observers around a plain white table, on which a luminous image was projected by a lens above in the roof. By rotating the lens around, the "camera" casts on the table a periscopic view of the surrounding scene.

In other words, the camera began as a theater, bigger even than a mainframe computer. In the case of *camera lucida* (a light room), cameras project an image on paper as an aid to sketching or drawing. Made in the shape of a cone with a lens and a reflecting mirror or prism at the apex and a drawing table inside, these devices allowed painters to trace out a sketch of the scene. At an opening on one side of the "camera" the artist sits, partly enveloped by a dark curtain. The camera lucida caused a small media scandal in 2002 when the *New York Times* revealed that several great artists used this crutch as the first step in their painting.

Technological advance eventually banished the artist from the room, allowing considerable miniaturization and automation. Replacing him was a silver halide homunculus, a light-sensitive plate or film. In 1839, in Paris, came L. J. M. Daguerre and the daguerrotype, using actinic effects (the impact of radiant energy on certain metals) to create better images through chemistry. Imparting a distinctive jaundice or sepia look to these pictures were the vapors of iodine used in developing them.

With the daguerrotype and its descendents, the portrait photographer became a hooded hangman fixing stiff images of posed subjects. Despite letting the victims remain unhooded, this process inflicted a facial malady that might be called *rigor photos*, hardly distinguishable much of the time from the rigor mortis that has now befallen all the subjects of these otherwise benign attentions.

The sepia saga of portable "boxes," vaulted chambers, hooded hangmen, canopied cavities, arched little caves of light, chemical baths, emulsions, tripods, and films dwindled over the decades into sleek metal vessels, full of tiny lenses and mirrors, that could easily be held in two hands, and then into miniature Minoltas that could be held between two fingers of one hand. Now, in the pattern of the computer, the camera will shrink further onto a sliver of silicon and become sand cheap and common. Then it will diffuse across the network, often connected by wires. The final liberation will dispense with the wires, linking the one-chip silicon imagers through the air to storage facilities capable of holding their voluminous reports.

The future after Foveon will confine the old paradigm of vaulted "cameras" chiefly to images that cannot be seen. Still needing a curved protective chamber rather than a mostly bare microchip will be tools for semiconductor photolithography and etching, scanning electron tunneling microscopes, nuclear resonance imagers, Computerized Axial Tomography (CAT) scanners, X rays, and inspection machines for baggage and shipping containers. But even in these applications, the chip itself will increasingly bear lenses and other apparatus required for capturing high-resolution images wherever they are needed. Already available from National Semiconductor are chips in the form of pellets that are consumed orally by the user and which take a series of photographs of the esophagus, stomach, and intestines, and then are unceremoniously extruded and flushed along with other offal, having wirelessly transmitted their report.

Foveon can do for the camera what Intel did for the computer: Reduce it to a chip and make it ubiquitous. Dismantle it and disperse it across the network. Render it wireless, wanton, and waste-able. Then, as Moore's Law shrinks the actual imager to an ever-smaller portion of the chip—just as it relegated the CPU to an ever-smaller corner of the modern single-chip system—the Foveon device will assume ever-more functions. No longer merely a sensor, it will aim toward intelligence. It will evolve into a vision system. It will become something of an eye, something of a brain.

That is, it will no longer serve merely to reflect the visible aspects of the world. Attaining powers of recognition and pattern matching, it will identify movements, threats, anomalies, fingerprints, faces, scenarios, poisons, weapons. It will find defects in manufacturing processes and descry trends in ambient traffic. It will prevent automobile accidents by recognizing dangerous patterns. It will help the ornithologist find his rare bird, the hunter his dangerous beast, and the rescuer her lost child. It will baby-sit and house-sit.

It will be described as an enemy of privacy. But it will enable us to defend privacy against the muggers, rapists, and terrorists who would most brutally rend it. It will eliminate most false charges that rip open the privacy and smear the reputation of nonmuggers and nonrapists. It will allow us to take more risks in the knowledge that our fate can be observed—that doctors and police will more often be in reach and informed.

Today human beings have more privacy than ever. Through much of human history people lived in small towns economically difficult to escape, where repute remained at the mercy of rumor, and from time to time, delusionary vigilantes burned a witch or lynched an adulterer. The increasing ubiquity of imagers will empower us to document our lives and prove our innocence against false charges, protect ourselves against predators, and enable more reliable and just enforcement of laws.

MANY LONG-TERM challenges lie ahead for the industry and for Foveon. To save the databases of the world from diluvian exabytes of image data, pouring in everywhere from billions of high-resolution chips gushing pixels twenty-four hours a day, graphic intelligence must be distributed and localized just as computer intelligence was distributed and localized by the PC. Capable of still and motion coverage, the imagers will have to select their targets, identify their subjects, and interpret the scene. Rather than remitting endless raw files, Foveon's chip will necessarily move toward recognition and pattern matching, selectivity and signaling.

Ironically these roles will lure the company back toward the kind of neuroscientific missions that gave it birth in Carverland, when Max Delbrück burst in upon the young Carver Mead with a biological challenge, when Misha Mahowald created her first schematic of the retina, and when the band of brothers began their pursuit of brain science. Revived will be the challenges of intelligent imaging embodied in the neuromorphic devices and neural-network recognizers that the company pursued under Federico Faggin in its original incarnation as Synaptics.

In one of his freshman physics lectures, Richard Feynman explains how the retina develops in the embryo as an extrusion of brain tissue, with long fibers later growing back to link the eyes to the visual cortex. Through the retina, as Feynman quotes an unknown observer, "the brain has found a way to look out into the world." Thus the retina is a window not only outward into the realms of light but also inward into the life of the brain and "the whole problem of physiology."

It is the prime example of the "transducer physiology" that Mead studied with Delbrück. It is the key challenge of analog technology—the interface between the outside world and inside computation, the links between light and logic, sensation and thought. It addresses the ways in which analogies for the shapes of things arise in the brain. And it offers a new way to understand the analogies between retina and camera—the way that the computer can extrude photosensitive silicon and find a way to look out into the world.

LIKE THE RETINA, the Foveon camera must also find "long fibers" to link it back to its users and give the optical network a way to look out into the world. To be stored or transported, Foveon pictures must be converted to digital form. If Foveon imagers are to make their way into the hands of every hobbyist and onto every computer videoconferencing terminal and into every surveillance application, from convenience stores to airports, the pictures will require and endow an abundance of storewidth: voluminous storage linked to immense bandwidth.

The natural way to process images is optical. With much of the information in the world interpretable as images, transmitted as images across fiber-optic lines, and stored as images in digital video disks and image databases, much of the processing of the future world economy should move toward analog optics.

The first great optical technology exploiting the parallel advantage of light and image is wavelength division multiplexing. It is a wave network rather than a bit network. Exploiting the natural parallelism of light, the wave network combines many different "colors" of infrared radiation, each bearing the equivalent of billions of bits per second, on a single fiber thread the width of a human hair.

But why "billions of bits" if it is an analog system? The source of the superiority of the wave net is its indifference to content. An all-optical network can transmit any kind of information at all—analog or digital—without distortion; it does not have to convert its waves into any readable form until their destination. In all-optical wave networks, the different-colored streams pass down passive analog optical paths that perform in parallel all the functions of active switching and multiplexing done in serial digital form in mixed optical and electronic networks. Bit networks have to read the digital addresses on every packet at every point where traffic must be added or dropped.

Wave networks are self-addressed in the very colors of the light, the frequencies of the waves. Each frequency designates a different path to a particular terminal. Like a Foveon camera, WDM is an inherently analog system optimized for the defining and transmission of colors. It is a camera on a country. The fiber-optic wave network is not merely a communications medium. It is also an analog processing path at the heart of a still massively digital Internet.

Despite the optical depression of the early 2000s, the superiority of the wave network grows steadily. New systems in preparation bear as many as one thousand wavelengths. Current Corvis equipment represents an 11,000-fold advance in six years, a rate of well over four doublings every year. Parallelism pays. With more than 1,000 fibers now sheathed in a single cable and 1,000 wavelengths per fiber and 10 gigabits equivalent per wavelength, a single fiber installation will soon be able to carry over a petabit, more than a full day's worth of 2003 Internet traffic, in one second. Emerging will be a global Foveal economy, engaged in dense image traffic, teleconferencing in high resolution, with full exploitation of the parallel advantage of light and image.

As image-bearing wavelengths become asymptotically free, they will be wasted in unexpected ways, enabling global simulations and experiences and transcending the isolation of human beings in time and space. Counting the number of wavelengths needed to accommodate some extrapolation of current bandwidth consumption is tantamount to counting the number of computers needed in the mainframe world of 1960, or tabulating the number of steam engines needed to run mines and factories in 1790.

The continuing prevalence of the routine digital camera and the digital switch in fact represent a forced stopgap on the way to analog solutions that respond to the physics of the media. An image or a path, a surveiller or a map, a spectrographic calculator or a retinal recognizer, a routing scheme or a pattern matcher, none of these is intrinsically digital at all. In analog form, these calculations happen naturally and instantly. As Misha Mahowald explained to me on our long walk in the mountains of Pasadena, your ears and eyes do it constantly. "They do not even know it's hard."

By the inexorable evolution of the industry, Foveon's color imaging will become the analog first step in a long process of cerebration that will end in simulating ever larger reaches of the human brain and extending back over fibers into a new global consciousness suffused with color and light.

That was the original dream, and it is the continuing quest.

Glossary

Amplifier—A device for increasing the strength of an electrical signal by allowing a small force on a control element to govern a large force in the circuit. The proportion between the small force and the large force it controls is called the amplifier's gain. A hydraulic analogy is a faucet, in which the force on the handle controls the flow.

Analog—Giving a continuous electronic representation of an image, sound, or pressure, simulating it using all points on an electrical waveform (rather than translating it into digital **bits** and **bytes**). Rather than "crunching numbers" as **digital** devices do, analog devices imitate real-world inputs in electrical form. Examples are film cameras, watches with hands to indicate the time, ordinary television sets, and human eyes and ears. Nearly all computers employ digital representations and then convert them to analog for observation by mostly analog humans.

Analog-to-digital converter (ADC)—A device for converting analog inputs into digital outputs. Compare **digital-to-analog converter (DAC)**, which converts digital inputs to analog outputs.

Aperture—A hole admitting light. It is measured as the effective diameter of a lens, usually translated in photography as the ratio of **focal length** to aperture diameter, familiar as the **f-number** of a lens.

Bayer pattern—A prevalent **mosaic** with two times as many green filters as red or blue filters, a proportion that correlates with human retinal sensitivities. It was invented by Bryce Bayer in 1976 and now is used in nearly all **digital** imagers, except Foveon's.

Bit—In information theory, the smallest unit of information, representing a zero or a one, on or off.

Black lipid bilayer—Synthetic chemicals that function identically to biological membranes, which sheathe nerves in "bilayers" and both protect cells and interface to other cells. Carver Mead used these substances in experiments comparing communications across **nerve channels** with communication across **transistors**.

Broca's Area—A region in the left frontal lobe of the brain that is active in the formation of language.

Byte—Eight **bits**.

Capacitor—An electrical device analogous to a ham sandwich, consisting of two conductors (bread slices) separated by an insulator (ham) that can briefly store an electrical charge or hold up the flow of a **current**. A ubiquitous electronic element used in dynamic memory cells to store a bit, in touch pads to identify movement of a finger, in microphones to transmit a sound, and in converters of direct current (DC) to alternating current (AC).

Charge-coupled device (CCD)—A silicon imager specialized for the reception of light intensities. It consists of a grid of light-sensitive **capacitors** that collect electric charge and couple to neighboring capacitors in a chain that delivers an image to a memory in a serial stream of **pixel** values.

Complementary metal oxide semiconductor (CMOS)—The basic design of most microchip circuits, combining two complementary **transistors** with a single input. When one transistor is turned on by an electrical charge, the other is turned off. At any one time at least half the transistors are off, thus saving power.

Cone—A light detector in the **retina** that registers brightness at moderate-to-high illumination levels. Cones come in three forms, to encode trichromatic color with their broad and smooth but differing sensitivities to the wavelengths of light. The retina contains 6 million cones (and 120 million **rods**).

Current—Electrical flow, measured in amperes ("amps"), analogous to water current in hydraulic systems.

Die—A single unpackaged **semiconductor** device. When it acquires its plastic or ceramic package and pins or other connectors, it becomes a microchip or just "chip." Its plural is also **die**.

Digital—Numerical representation—based on **bits** and **bytes**—that uses only two points on a waveform or two positions on a switch (on or off) to convey numerical information. Digital computers are known as "number crunchers."

Digital signal processor (DSP)—A silicon processor that performs fast multiplication and accumulation functions, which enable it to handle signals, such as audio and video, in real time as they arrive, and convert them into a form suitable for display or transmission. DSPs perform much of the work in **digital** cameras, where they transform a digital stream of light measurements into a usable image.

Digital subscriber line (DSL)—Method of using an ordinary copper phone line to send between 200 kilobits per second and 8 megabits per second, or in advanced systems up to 52 megabits per second.

Digital-to-analog converter (DAC)—See **analog-to-digital converter**.

Fan-in—Number of inputs that a device can receive. Inbound connectivity.

Fan-out—Number of outputs a device can transmit. Outbound connectivity.

Flash memory—The memory technology commonly used to store images in a digital camera. A non**volatile memory** chip that stores values on an array of insulated capacitors called "floating gates" because they represent an island of capacitance "floating" in a silicon dioxide insulator with no active or leaky connections to the circuitry of the memory grid on the chip. They are read or written by exotic quantum "tunneling" or "avalanche" effects.

Flux capacitor—An imaginary device in Steven Spielberg's film *Back to the Future* that was alleged to enable time travel. The name, however, accurately describes the memory cell in a computer memory chip called a dynamic random access memory, or DRAM, in which electric charge is in constant flux in **capacitors** connected to a microscopic grid of wires by **transistors**. **CCD** cells also might be termed flux capacitors.

F-number—The ratio of the **focal length** of a lens to the diameter of its **aperture**. The smaller the f-number the larger the aperture and the more light enabled to pass. Maximum aperture (low f-number) is a rough index of lens quality.

Focal length—Gauges the distance between a calculable point in a lens and that point of focus where the image is sharpest. Focal lengths are measured in millimeters. Small focal lengths mean wide-angle lenses, while large focal lengths are associated with telephoto lenses. In most lenses, focal lengths are fixed, but variable focal-length lenses, called "zooms," are increasingly effective and popular. Together with the size of the **imager's** light-sensitive area, the focal length determines a camera's field of view: the picture. A short focal length reduces or compresses the size of the image projected onto the sensor, resulting in more of the scene being captured in a given sensor area, thereby increasing the field of view. An increased sensor area will also increase the field of view. Thus the benefits of reducing the size of **pixels**, or of **imagers**, are limited.

Fovea—The part of the retina dedicated to high-resolution color vision, and the inspiration for the company name Foveon. It is an indented area composed of a dense array of **cones** directly behind the eye's lens, where it is obstructed by less nerve tissue than other parts of the retina. The fovea distinguishes detailed lineaments and colors in an image, such as words on a page or features of a face in a crowd. When you focus on an image directly in front of your eyes, you are using your fovea, but it doesn't work in conditions of low illumination, because it has no rods.

Fry's—A famous chain of electronics stores in Silicon Valley, south of San Francisco.

Graphics Interchange Format (GIF)—A compression scheme for **digital** images, limited to 256 colors.

Imager—In **digital** cameras, a device for detecting light and measuring its frequency (color), intensity (energy in photons), and location on a grid. The key component in a digital camera, it takes the form of a **charge-coupled device** or a **CMOS** chip. In most **analog** cameras the imager is essentially film.

Ion—A charged atom or molecule having gained (anion) or lost (cation) one or more of its outside band of electrons, which determine its chemical behavior. The **nerve channels** of the brain communicate electrically by ionic conduction.

JPEG—Developed by the Joint Photographics Expert Group, JPEG is widely used to designate a method of compression of **digital** still images for transfer or display, but because it is lossy (it loses information), JPEG is unsuitable for medical images where the details must be exactly accurate. The compression ratio can be as high as 40 to 1.

Microprocessor—A **digital** computing device inscribed on a **silicon** microchip and providing the "central processing unit" (CPU) in a personal computer or an embedded processing unit in other kinds of equipment such as cameras. Microprocessors are mostly **von Neumann machines**.

Mosaic (also known as color filter mosaic [CFM] or color filter array [CFA])—An array of color filters, typically a **Bayer pattern**, superimposed on the imager of a **digital** camera, in order give color to black-and-white imagers. Mosaics restrict each pixel to a single one of the three primary colors (red, green, and blue). Although it is said that mosaics reproduce the performance of **cones** in the eye, cones in humans respond to all three colors, though in different degrees, much as the three stacked receptors in a Foveon imager do.

Nanometer—One billionth of a meter. Ten silicon atoms in a row would be roughly a nanometer wide. The wavelengths of light are between about 400 nanometers (violet) and 700 nanometers (red).

Nerve channel—An elongated biological cell through which signals are passed as a result of differences in electrical or **ionic** charge across the cell's membrane. It is analogous to a wire in a computer.

Nerve membrane—A sheath consisting of fatty molecules called phospholipids surrounding a nerve cell. It both protects cells and interfaces to other cells. It is analogous but not electrically similar to the silicon dioxide layer on a **silicon** chip that both insulates the device electrically and protects it chemically.

Neural network—A network of artificial **neurons** or **neurodes** used as a computer system. Based on a cartoon image of the processing functions of a brain, some neural networks can outperform ordinary **von Neumann** computers in functions of pattern matching or signal processing such as imaging or speech recognition.

Neurode—A simulated **neuron** used in a **neural network**. It sums inputs, using a threshhold level as a nonlinear trigger for decision making.

Neuron—One of the processing cells of a brain. According to various estimates by neuroscientists, the human brain has between ten billion and a hundred billion neurons. In other words, they still don't have much of a clue.

Nonvolatile memory—A form of memory that does not lose its contents when the power goes out. Popular nonvolatile memories include **flash** and disk drives. Compare **Volatile memory**.

Phase—The timing of an electromagnetic wave or point in its progress (often signified by the angle that it subtends on a 360-degree circular graph depicting the wave as a rotation around the graph). Two waves in phase will add their amplitudes (crests); to the degree two waves are out of phase, they interfere destructively (the troughs will tend to nullify the crests).

In chemistry, however, **phase** signifies the condition of the element. For example, the three phases of H_2O are fluid, gaseous, and frozen (water, steam, and ice).

Physical layer—The bottom level of a seven-layer model of electronic and communications equipment, comprising the physical hardware, such as the **silicon** microchip or **silica** fiber-optic line. Above the physical layer are six levels of "firmware" and software, ending with the application, such as Word or Photoshop, that performs the computer function by controlling the lower layers.

Pixel—Short for "picture element." The information from one spot in an image, or one photodetector in an **imager**, conceived as a dense array or matrix of spots or photodetectors. **Digital** cameras commonly measure their resolution in megapixels (millions of pixels), but actual resolution is determined not by the number of spots but by the quality, accuracy, and arrangement of the information delivered from the spots.

Polysilicon—Noncrystalline or amorphous **silicon** used for wires on chips. Federico Faggin's **silicon gate** was in fact polysilicon.

Quantum theory—The theory of the interactions between matter on the atomic scale and light or other electromagnetic waveforms. Combining waves and particles in apparently paradoxical ways, quantum theory doesn't make "sense," but it is mathematically coherent. It is the theory of the *microcosm* of invisible phenomena as distinguished from the *macrocosm* of visible things governed by Newton's laws or relativity theory.

Retina—A densely connected three-layer array of **neurons** at the back of the eye that gauges the intensity and color of incident light and sends the measurements to the optic nerve, which passes them on to the cortex where they are formed into an image.

Rod—Light detector in the **retina** that registers brightness at very low levels of illumination, as for night vision. The retina contains 120 million rods but only 6 million **cones**, suggesting that the human race evolved mainly in the dark.

Semiconductor—An element, such as **silicon**, that can be readily adapted either to pass or to block **current** by doping its surface with appropriate **ions** and applying a **voltage** or current. Semiconductors thus can be made into **solid-state** electronic switches.

Silica—**Silicon** oxide, usually encountered as glass or quartz.

Silicon—Pure crystalline sand used in microchips. The second most common element in the Earth's crust behind oxygen (mixed with silicon in the microchip's silicon-dioxide insulating layer) and ahead of aluminum (bauxite) used in most wires on the microchip's surface.

Silicon gate—The part of a **CMOS transistor** that controls the flow of electricity through the circuit. Analogous to the base in a bipolar transistor. Previously made of metal, the gate region was first converted to silicon in practical devices by Federico Faggin at Fairchild Semiconductor Corporation and at Intel following a concept pioneered at Bell Laboratories.

Single lens reflex (SLR)—An expensive professional camera that enables a photographer to control the functions of the camera manually.

Solid state—The physics of solid materials such as **semiconductors**.

T-1 line—A telephone company service combining 24 64-kilobit voice-oriented phone lines into a single 1.544-megabits-per-second data connection. T-1 lines are now often rendered by **DSL**.

Transducer—A mostly **analog** device that changes a signal from one form to another without altering its essential value. Eyes, ears, sensors, photodetectors, and other devices interfacing between the real world and its symbolic representations or among different representations are transducers.

Transistor—A "transfer resistor" or device that controls the flow of relatively large electrical **currents** by varying the **voltage** or current on its "gate" or "base." It can function either as an **analog amplifier** or as a **digital** switch. A modern digital microchip contains millions of transistors, but analog transistors are often discrete (one or several in a package). Putting hundreds of thousands of analog transistors on a single microchip for sensory functions was the revolutionary idea of Carver Mead that led to Foveon.

Unix—A computer operating system invented at Bell Labs in 1969 by a team led by Ken Thompson and Dennis Richie. Designed as a single-user version of MIT's multiuser Multics, Unix has become the dominant operating system for powerful workstation computers.

Visible light—Wavelengths between 400 and 700 **nanometers** and frequencies between 430 and 750 **terahertz** (trillions of hertz or cycles per second). The portion of the electromagnetic spectrum that registers on the **cones** of the **retina** in the human eye and is not deemed by influential phobics to cause cancer. A one over 10,000,000,000,000,000,000,000,000 (10^{24}) portion of the total electromagnetic spectrum.

VLSI—Very Large Scale Integration, a phrase used in the microchip industry to designate devices with more than a few score thousand **transistors**. Essentially all today's **digital** microchips are VLSI, which remains in more common use in describing chips with scores of millions of transistors than the technically accurate ULSI (Ultra Large Scale Integration). Carver Mead developed design techniques for creating VLSI circuits and then developed **analog** VLSI devices that can interface directly with real-world sounds, images, pressures, and other phenomena.

Volatile memory—Memory that requires a power source in order to retain its content. Contrast **Nonvolatile memory**. The most common volatile memories are the dynamic random access memory (DRAM) and static random access memory (SRAM).

Voltage—Electrical pressure, analogous to water pressure in hydraulic systems. Measured in volts.

von Neumann machine—A computer architecture in which the same storage devices hold both the software program and the data. With a single path between the processor and the memory, holding both instructions and data, von Neumann machines tend to be characterized by the *von Neumann bottleneck*. That is, the bulk of the time of the computation is consumed in the process of moving instructions and data in a "Step 'n' Fetchit" manner to and from memory locations according to a regular clock or counter. Although many efforts have been made to transcend this architecture—in particular **neural networks**—nearly all the billions of computer devices in the world are still essentially von Neumann machines.

Wafer—A **silicon** disk, typically either 200 or 300 millimeters in diameter (8 or 12 inches) potentially holding hundreds of **die**. The wafer is *diced* into die.

Wafer fab—A chip factory, often called simply a "fab."

Acknowledgments

The path to this book began twenty years ago, when in the course of writing *Wealth and Poverty* I encountered the microchip industry and devoted a chapter to it. The researches for that chapter later inspired a book called *The Spirit of Enterprise* that then broke into two books. One, now available as *Recapturing the Spirit of Enterprise*, was on entrepreneurship. It centered on Micron corporation, a tiny team of chip designers in Boise, Idaho, who were challenging the Japanese establishment in the production of memory chips at a time when savvy industry observers believed that the industry had moved inexorably to Asia. Fifteen years later, Micron reigned as the world's leading memory chip company. The second book was called *Microcosm*. It explored the history and consequences of the move of industry from the visible mechanical realm into the invisible domains of quantum physics.

The Silicon Eye combines the themes of *Microcosm* and *The Spirit of Enterprise*. It tells the story of a small entrepreneurial company in Silicon Valley that is challenging the Japanese camera and imager establishment at a time when most experts think that this industry has followed much of the microchip industry in moving inexorably to Asia.

Starting as part of Synaptics Corporation in the early 1990s, the imager project spun off into Foveon in 1996. Employing the silicon technology of the microcosm, both Foveon and Synaptics are engaged in an effort to forge interconnections between the world of visible things and the invisible world of the microcosm, between sensory phenomena and insensate computation. *The Silicon Eye* tells the story of how scientists and engineers have addressed this sensory and biological domain of sight and touch and hearing and linked it to the ever-expanding world of microchips.

The scientific leader in this journey is Carver Mead, formerly the Gordon and Betty Moore Professor of Science and Engineering at Caltech. I first met him twenty years ago in the restaurant of the Marriott Hotel at the Newark, New Jersey, Airport, where he was staying during a trip devoted to teaching his new chip design techniques to the microchip division of Bell Labs. I quickly discovered that he is the world's best teacher of the interplay between the physics of microchips and the larger world of engineering systems. Without his constant guidance, wise and persistent teaching, and inspiring counsel, my career as a technology analyst would have been impossible and *The Silicon Eye* could not have been written.

In subsequent years, I became a frequent visitor to Caltech, attending lectures in Carver's classroom, meeting his students, and studying with them. Among the students who helped me most during this period were Misha Mahowald and David Gillespie, both of whom play crucial roles in this book. Mead also introduced me to Richard Lyon, who was helping him teach his course on chip design. I spent many hours both with Misha and with Dick learning the intricacies of their science.

In the early 1990s, at a conference on the biological origins of economics based on Michael Rothchild's book *Bionomics*, I met Federico Faggin for the first time. Already a legend in the Valley as the creator of the first microprocessors at Intel, Faggin told of the promise of the new company, Synaptics, that he had launched in part to pursue the ideas of Carver Mead. Faggin led Synaptics into world leadership in touch pads for mobile computers and other devices. As chairman of Synaptics, Mead ended up attracting many of his ex-students to the company. Faggin and his wife, Alvia, a technology journalist, were unfailingly helpful and attentive in the course of my research for this book.

In telling the story of Synaptics, Tim Allen and David Gillespie offered extensive interviews, documentary support, and valuable personal insights. Recounting the saga of the early years of Foveon as it emerged from Synaptics, Tobi Delbrück and Nick Mascarenhas were crucial. Delbrück also gave a critical reading to the book. Dick Merrill and Dick Lyon were indispensable in explaining the intricacies of Foveon's technology. In telling the story of the charge-coupled device, I relied heavily on Bob Johnstone's pathbreaking text *We Were Burning: Japanese Entrepreneurs and the Forging of the Electronic Age*.

From Atlas Books and W. W. Norton, Jim Atlas and Jesse Cohen proved to be book doctors who make house calls, visiting me at home in the Berkshires to give me the kind of detailed and sophisticated editorial attention that is said to be rare in contemporary publishing. At the Discovery Institute in Seattle, where I serve as a senior fellow, my old friend Bruce Chapman gave me continual aid and encouragement as I worked my way through this project. At the Gilder Technology Report, Nick Tredennick, Bret Swanson, Mary Collins, and Charles Burger all offered constant support and insights. Sandy Fleischmann became a master of the Sigma camera and maintained our technology forum at www.gildertech.com. Tom Owens and Tina Chase kept the business going while I wrote the book. Andy Kessler, the author of *Wall Street Meat* and *Running Money*, improved my early draft with an astute critique. Former MIT professor and now business magnate Larry Sweet provided a valuable early reading and a more rigorous definition of crucial terms than I could use here. The first and most transformative editor of the book was my daughter Louisa, herself the author of a forthcoming work on the physics of quantum entanglement.

My wife, Nini, is at the source and center of all I do.

—George Gilder

January 10, 2005

Index